Exploring TEXAS with Children

Sharry Buckner

Republic of Texas Press

Republic of Texas Press is an imprint of Wordware Publishing, Inc.
No part of this book may be reproduced in any form or by
any means without permission in writing from
Wordware Publishing, Inc.

Printed in the United States of America

ISBN 1-55622-624-1
10 9 8 7 6 5 4 3 2 1
9811

All inquiries for volume purchases of this book should be addressed to
Wordware Publishing, Inc., at 2320 Los Rios Boulevard, Plano, Texas
75074. Telephone inquiries may be made by calling:

(972) 423-0090

To Al, my companion on the trails, and to James and Jennifer, my grandchildren who I wish lived closer so I could explore the endearing Texas backroads with them.

Contents

Contents

Hill Country

North Central

North East

Contents

South Central

South East

South & Gulf Coast

Contents

INTRODUCTION

Texas is BIG. Huge. Vast. Exactly 267,277 square miles vast. The only way to see it is in small bits and pieces. The diversity of climate, geography, ethnic population, and history is almost beyond comprehension to those who have never been here. For those of you just traveling through, this book can help you find things to enjoy along your route. For those of you who live in the Lone Star State, it can be a guide to mini-vacations and weekend getaways as well as extended vacations. Or use it as a guide to entertain children who come to visit.

Exploring Texas with Children presents a selection of places children will enjoy in Texas. "Children" encompasses young people from toddlers to teenagers, who, of course, frequently enjoy different kinds of activities. This book gives enough description to decide if your family will enjoy the attractions mentioned. It covers mainly the backroads and small towns and should complement other books in the series, including *Exploring Dallas with Children* and *Exploring San Antonio with Children*.

Local places to eat and stay offer special experiences for families. Be sure to try chicken-fried steak, Texas Bar-B-Q (barbecue), Tex-Mex food, and German sausages and pastries at the quaint "Mom and Pop" eateries along the way.

For valuable planning information, see the resources listed in the appendix at the end of the book. And have a great journey!

Sharry

The prices and hours of operations listed in this guide-book were confirmed at press time. However, we recommend that you call to obtain current information.

Two Travel Tips

This book does not attempt to instruct how to travel with children—there are excellent books that do that in depth (see the resources pages). However, I will mention two of my favorite ideas—a pre-trip activity and a post-trip one.

- Encourage the kids to help plan the vacation. Let the children send off or call or e-mail for free tourist brochures and maps from the places you'll be visiting. *Exploring Texas with Children* lists addresses and toll-free phone numbers of Convention and Visitors Bureaus for most cities, as well as addresses for major attractions. Schedule a "vacation planning" day or evening and spread everything out on the dining room table. A friend has had great success by letting each child pick three things he/she would like to do or see. This, of course, can vary depending on the time available and number and ages of children. Adapt the idea to fit your family's situation. Remember to stay loose enough for spur-of-the-moment activities.

- Make a scrapbook when you get home. Let the kids gather items along the way to be included: ticket stubs, postcards, photos, brochures, and other memorabilia. Let each child choose a specific item to collect. The whole family will enjoy making the scrapbook, and it will provide fond memories for years to come.

Panhandle

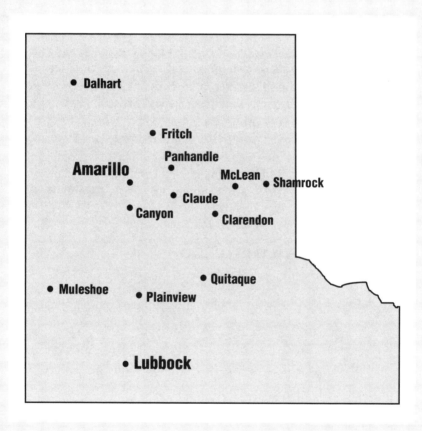

- Dalhart
- Fritch
- Panhandle
- Amarillo
- McLean
- Shamrock
- Claude
- Canyon
- Clarendon
- Quitaque
- Muleshoe
- Plainview
- Lubbock

AMARILLO

see also: CANYON
Convention & Visitors Council
1000 S. Polk St.
800-692-1338 or 806-374-1497
http://www.amarillo-cvb.org

Amarillo (Spanish for "yellow") is the commercial, cultural, and recreational center for the vast region known as the Texas Panhandle. You'll see lots of wide-open spaces and breathtaking sunsets, and feel the rich western heritage. Old Route 66 passes through town and attracts thousands of visitors who enjoy a nostalgic trip to that era of American history. Throughout the city are 56 parks that cover over 2,300 acres and offer recreational facilities such as swimming pools, tennis courts, playgrounds, fishing lakes, and a 36-hole municipal golf course. Amarillo is also the gateway to Palo Duro Canyon, America's second largest canyon (see Canyon).

AMARILLO ZOO
806-381-7911

See a herd of bison roaming a 20-acre range, other animals of the High Plains, and a special "Texotic" exhibit.

Location: N.E. 24th St. at U.S. 287 in Thompson Park

Hours: Tuesday - Sunday 9:30 a.m. - 5:00 p.m.

Admission: FREE

AMERICAN QUARTER HORSE HERITAGE CENTER AND MUSEUM

806-376-5181

Ever wonder what a jockey sees? Experience a jockey's eye-view on horseback from the starting gates! This world-class facility offers many hands-on and interactive exhibits, video presentations, and live demonstrations about the history and significance of the American Quarter Horse. Watch the fascinating orientation show, which uses the latest laser disc technology and finest sound system available, in the 70-seat theater. The exciting presentation combines action, music, and lighting to show the development and history of the breed.

Visit the stable, where you can watch brief video tapes—"Fella," a talking horse, tells how to buy and care for your own American Quarter Horse. Sit in authentic saddle seats in the Performance Theater with its choice of six videos. Visit the special play area for little ones. A full-size cutaway horse trailer displays the equipment used by American Quarter Horse Youth Association members in shows. This extraordinary facility also includes the American Quarter Horse Hall of Fame, a vast research library and archives (open by appointment), excellent gift shop, and meeting rooms.

Location: 2601 I-40 East (I-40 at Quarter Horse Drive)

Hours: May 1 - Labor Day: Monday - Saturday 9:00 a.m. - 5:00 p.m., Sunday noon - 5:00 p.m.; after Labor Day - April 30: Tuesday - Saturday 10:00 a.m. - 5:00 p.m.; closed New Year's Day, Thanksgiving, Christmas Eve, and Christmas Day

Admission: $4/adults, $3.50/seniors, $2.50/children 6-18, children under 6 free

CADILLAC RANCH

Dubbed "the hood ornament of Route 66" by one of its creators, this one-of-a-kind attraction consists of ten vintage Cadillacs buried nose-down in a field at the same angle as Cheops' pyramids.

Location: About seven miles west of Amarillo on the south side of I-40 (between Helium and Hope exits)

COWBOY MORNING AND EVENING

800-658-2613 or 806-944-5562

Yummmmm! Imagine eating Texas eggs, ranch sausage, sourdough biscuits, and skillet gravy in the cool morning air under the wide Texas sky. You can do just that at this Old West-style chuckwagon breakfast at the Figure 3 Ranch "campsite" perched on the rim of Palo Duro Canyon. A 20-minute ride across the prairie in mule-drawn wagons takes you there. Smell the tantalizing aroma of the genuine cowboy meal cooked over an open mesquite fire. Then sit back and sample the cowpoke life— branding, roping, and cowchip tossing.

If you're not an "early-bird," go for the Cowboy Dinner and feast on the same famous sourdough biscuits with sizzling Texas-sized steaks, hot pinto beans, salad, and campfire cobbler. The ending scene of *Indiana Jones and the Last Crusade* was filmed at this authentic working ranch.

Hours: April - October (daily from June - August). Breakfast at 8:30 a.m. Dinner times vary. By reservation only.

Admission: Cowboy Morning $19/adult, $14.50/children 4-12, children under 4 free

Cowboy Evening: $22.50/adult, $14.50/children 4-12, children under 4 free

4

Cowboy Morning
Photo courtesy of Amarillo Convention & Visitors Council

DON HARRINGTON DISCOVERY CENTER

806-355-9547
http://www.dhdc.org

Located in the center of a 51-acre park with a lake, two play-grounds, walking trail, and picnic area, this center offers over one hundred exhibits and attractions that encourage hands-on activity. The Exploration Gallery explores the physical sciences and the laws of nature, the Construction Zone demonstrates how and why structures work, another wing features the earth and life sciences, and Kidscovery is a special area for preschoolers. "Aquariums of the World" feature fish from exotic waters. All varieties of programs and workshops are continuing events.

And special events are really that. The annual outdoor Labor Day concert and fireworks display attracts more than 50,000 people. The planetarium has awesome night sky programs—you'll travel through space with the help of 200 special effects projectors and a 360 degree hemispheric projector.

Location: 1200 Streit Dr.

Hours: Tuesday - Saturday 10:00 a.m. - 5:00 p.m., Sunday 1:00 - 5:00 p.m.; closed major holidays. Weekend planetarium shows September - May, daily June-August.

Admission: $3 fee for planetarium shows

HELIUM MONUMENT

This six-story stainless steel time column was erected in 1968, adjacent to the Don Harrington Discovery Center. It commemorates the world's greatest quantity of helium, a natural element, which is found here. Yes, that's what balloons are filled with.

ROUTE 66

Get your kicks on Route 66! Look for the "Old Route 66" highway signs marking the course through the city. Buildings that once housed theaters, cafes, and drug stores are now quaint antique, craft, and specialty shops, and unique restaurants along "Old San Jacinto," one mile of the historic route, on Sixth Street between Georgia and Western Streets. Several books and guides are available to lead you to the sights and memories along the route.

WONDERLAND AMUSEMENT PARK

800-383-4712 or 806-383-3344
http://www.wonderlandpark.com

Ride the "Texas Tornado," one of the top-rated double-loop steel roller coasters in the country. One of Texas' largest privately owned amusement parks, Wonderland features 25 rides, including the Big Splash log flume, Fantastic Journey spook house, Raging Rapids water slide, bumper cars, miniature golf, arcades, and food concessions.

Location: U.S. 287 North at River Road exit

Hours: Vary

Admission: $8.95 weekdays, $14.95 weekends (all-inclusive)

BIG TEXAN STEAK RANCH AND OPRY

800-657-7177 or 806-372-6000

Everybody wants a free meal! The Big Texan is known far and wide for its 72-ounce steak dinner offered free to anyone who can eat the steak and all the trimmings in one hour. Here's your chance to try rattlesnake or calf fries. The restaurant is stuffed with western memorabilia and is a fun place to people-watch, especially if you're near someone trying to eat the free dinner. Kids will love the Big Time Arcade, parents will enjoy the Big Time Gift Shop, and everyone enjoys the Tuesday night Big Texas Opry featuring performances by a variety of country-western entertainers.

Location: I-40 at Lakeside

Canyon

see also: Amarillo
Convention & Visitors Bureau
800-999-9481

 Palo Duro Canyon State Park
800-792-1112 (State Park information)
806-488-2227 (Ranger Station)
http://www.tpwd.state.tx.us/park/parks.htm

Prairie grass and flatlands stretch as far as you can see, until the landscape breaks abruptly about 25 miles southeast of Amarillo into the vast chasm of Palo Duro Canyon. On this expansive terrain of the Texas High Plains, the Prairie Dog Town fork of the Red River has carved surprising spires and pinnacles.

Palo Duro Canyon
Photo courtesy of Amarillo Convention & Visitors Council

Walls plunge a thousand feet to the canyon floor, exposing brilliant multicolored strata and geological formations paralleled in beauty only by the Grand Canyon.

The 16-mile park road offers visitors only a taste of the rugged beauty of one of Texas' largest state parks (16,402 acres). It winds through an unfurling panorama carved by millions of years of wind and water erosion. To see more of the scenic landscapes, ride mountain bikes, hike the trails, or ride horses off the beaten paths. The park has first-class facilities, campsites for tents and RVs, picnic areas, miles of hiking trails; also riding stables and mountain bike rentals.

Location: About 12 miles east of Canyon via Texas 217 and Park Rd. 5

Admission: Entrance fee, camping fee

"TEXAS" MUSICAL DRAMA

806-655-2181

Look up! Horsemen carrying flags appear atop the 600-foot canyon bluff as colorfully costumed singers and dancers sweep across the stage below. Both kids and adults love "TEXAS," a spectacular outdoor drama performed in the 1,500-seat Pioneer Amphitheater in Palo Duro Canyon State Park. Period costumes, dynamic dancing, and vibrant voices tell the settlers' stories of romance and humor, struggles, and strengths. This musical extravaganza uses a professional cast of eighty to recapture the drama of Panhandle history.

The spectacular sound effects and remarkable lighting against a natural backdrop under the bright Texas stars add to the excitement. Free parking, reserved seats, restrooms, drinks, snacks, souvenirs, tapes, and photographs are available at the theatre. A barbecue dinner is served in the area before every performance for an additional charge. Advance tickets are highly recommended.

Location: In Palo Duro Canyon State Park

Mailing address for advance tickets: P.O. Box 268, Canyon, TX 79115

Hours: Presentations nightly except Sundays from late June through late August

"TEXAS" musical drama
Photo courtesy of "TEXAS"

PANHANDLE-PLAINS HISTORICAL MUSEUM

806-656-2244
http://www.wtamu.edu/museum/home.html

Experience the stories of courage, of hardship, of victory and defeat of the early pioneers and settlers . . . all told through a variety of interpretive exhibits. Some detail the daily lives of cowboys on Panhandle ranches. The original T-Anchor Ranch House, constructed in the late 1870s, has been reconstructed on the Museum grounds, complete with outbuildings and windmill.

Follow the board sidewalks of Pioneer Town and take a look at life in a small Panhandle settlement at the turn of the century. Wonder at how your ancestors got around in buggies, sleighs, and wagons from the nineteenth century. Automobiles from 1900 through the 1950s are also displayed. Travel through a simulated tunnel with oil well drilling tools at work and emerge to find a 1920s oil and gas field with a working pump jack. Learn how oil people lived and worked and see the technology of those times. Or meet a life-size, meat-eating Allosaurus, ground sloth, sabre-toothed cat, and shovel-tusked mastodon, all on display in the Paleontology section.

The Panhandle-Plains Historical Museum is the oldest and largest state-supported historical museum in Texas, and it is really five museums in one (petroleum, western heritage, paleontology, transportation, and art), housing over 3½ million artifacts in approximately 300,000 square feet. Built in 1933, the Texas limestone structure features decorative stone work and carvings on its facade. The building bears a State Antiquities Landmark designation awarded for its unique Art Deco architectural style.

Location: 2401 Fourth Ave. on the West Texas A&M University campus

Hours: June - August: Monday - Saturday 9:00 a.m. - 6:00 p.m., Sunday 1:00 - 6:00 p.m.; September - May: Monday - Saturday

9:00 a.m. - 5:00 p.m., Sunday 1:00 - 6:00 p.m.; closed New Year's Day, Thanksgiving Day, Christmas Eve, Christmas Day.

Admission: $4/adults, $3/seniors, $1/children ages 4-12

CLARENDON

BAR H DUDE RANCH

800-627-9871 or 806-874-2634
http://www.tourtexas.com/barhduderanch/

Stay on a working Texas dude ranch! Here you can join in with ranch chores or sit back and relax, go horseback riding, or swim in season. Enjoy chuckwagon dinners and campfires.

Location: Texas FM 3257, off U.S. 287, three miles from Clarendon.

CLAUDE

SCENIC DRIVE

One of the most impressive scenic drives in the state goes from Claude near Amarillo, south on TX 207 to Silverton. Miles of plains and wheat fields sweep from horizon to horizon until suddenly the highway plunges into the scenic splendor of Palo Duro Canyon. Farther south the highway drops into another beautiful gorge, Tule Canyon, with even more varieties of rock strata and sheer-faced, knife-edged buttes.

DALHART

XIT RANCH AND MUSEUM

Can you imagine a ranch of three million acres? That's 3,000,000 acres! This entire area was once part of the famous XIT Ranch, the world's largest fenced ranch in the 1880s. See a wealth of exhibits including railroad antiques, Indian artifacts, frontier fire-arms, cowboy clothing, and saddles and tack at the XIT Museum. You can also try to imagine life in those days in the completely furnished kitchen, parlour, and bedroom from the turn of the century.

Location: 108 E. Fifth St.

Hours: Monday - Saturday 9:00 a.m. - 5:00 p.m.

FRITCH

ALIBATES FLINT QUARRIES NATIONAL MONUMENT

806-857-3151
http://www.nps.gov/alfl/

Ancient Indians began mining these quarries for flint as far back as 10,000 B.C., and the mining didn't slow down until the 1800s. Alibates flint, renowned for its varied colors, occurs in the Canadian River breaks near Fritch and Amarillo. This multicolored flint was highly prized in ancient times for making weapons and tools. Today visitors can take a park ranger-guided walking tour through the quarries. Collecting flint specimens is prohibited.

> Alibates Flint Quarries is the only National Monument in Texas.

Location: Highway 136, south of Fritch, turn west at Lake Meredith Recreational Area, about 5½ miles to the ranger station

Hours: Tours conducted daily Memorial Day - Labor Day at 10:00 a.m. and 2:00 p.m.

Admission: FREE

LAKE MEREDITH AQUATIC AND WILDLIFE MUSEUM
806-857-2458

This remarkable museum contains some excellent wildlife dioramas depicting American eagles, wild turkeys, pronghorns, coyotes, deer, and raccoons. A National Park Service display shows a wide variety of colors of Alibates flint that the Indians used to make arrowheads and tools. The aquarium focuses on the marine life of nearby Lake Meredith.

Hours: Tuesday - Friday 10:00 a.m. - 5:00 p.m., Saturday 9:00 a.m. - 5:00 p.m., Sunday 2:00 - 5:00 p.m.; closed New Year's Day, Christmas Day, Thanksgiving Day

Admission: FREE

LAKE MEREDITH NATIONAL RECREATION AREA
806-857-3151
http://www.nps.gov/lamr/

The 16,500-acre lake and recreation area is operated by the National Park Service and offers camping areas, shelters, restrooms, fishing, swimming, boat ramps, docks, and marina service.

LUBBOCK

Lubbock Convention & Visitors Bureau
14th and Avenue K
800-692-4035 or 806-747-5232
http://www.lubbocklegends.com

The town that gave the world Buddy Holly has surprising diversity in its attractions. Lubbock offers culture and history with its ballet, several community theaters, and the fine museums of Texas Tech University. You'll find quaint shops and restaurants in the Depot District, amusement and water parks, and even an entertaining prairie dog town.

BUDDY HOLLY STATUE AND WALK OF FAME

Honoring its most famous son, Lubbock has created a larger-than-life bronze statue of Buddy Holly in a park bearing his name. Surrounding Buddy is the Walk of Fame honoring musicians and actors from Lubbock and West Texas, including Mac Davis, Waylon Jennings, Jimmy Dean, Tanya Tucker, Roy Orbison, Bob Wills, and the Gatlin brothers. Born in 1936, Buddy Holly had recorded over one hundred songs, including *Peggy Sue* and *Oh Boy* before a plane crash ended his short career at the age of twenty-two. The Buddy Holly festival in early September each year draws thousands of fans from around the world.

Location: Eighth St. and Ave. Q

MacKenzie Park: Joyland Amusement Park, Prairie Dog Town

806-763-2719 (Joyland)

What show-offs! The pint size rodent residents of Prairie Dog Town are natural showmen and entertain the whole family. One of the few remaining colonies of its type in the nation, Prairie

Dog Town is located in the heart of Lubbock's Mackenzie Park recreation area. The park also encompasses Meadowbrook Municipal Golf Course, and Joyland Amusement Park with twenty-three great rides, and food courts.

Location: I-27 at Fourth St.

Hours: Daily mid-May - mid-August; weekends spring and fall

MUSEUM OF TEXAS TECH UNIVERSITY AND MOODY PLANETARIUM

806-742-2490

This outstanding museum covers a broad range of arts, humanities, social sciences, and natural sciences with a special emphasis on southwestern history.

Location: Fourth St. and Indiana on the campus of Texas Tech University

Hours: Tuesday - Saturday 10:00 a.m. - 5:00 p.m. (Thursday until 8:30 p.m.), Sunday 1:00 - 5:00 p.m.

Admission: FREE

MOODY PLANETARIUM offers regular programs and a special outer space exhibit.

Hours: Program times: Tuesday - Friday at 3:30 p.m., Thursday at 7:30 p.m., Saturday and Sunday at 2:00 and 3:30 p.m.

Admission: $1/adults, 50¢/students, children and seniors free

RANCHING HERITAGE CENTER

806-742-2498
Tour information: 806-742-2456

Believe it or not, John Wayne and Clint Eastwood didn't portray the history of ranching in Texas and the American West exactly

as it was. See what it was really like at this extraordinary outdoor exhibit—the only one of its kind in America. More than
thirty authentic structures, most donated by ranchers, were
moved to this 15-acre site and reconstructed. A bunkhouse,
barn, blacksmith shop, windmill, ranch home, and schoolhouse
depict life in the nineteenth and twentieth centuries. See the
shipping pens and corrals and chuckwagon for a taste of the cowboy's life. All the buildings are exceptionally well restored and
furnished. Docents in period dress demonstrate such activities
as butter churning and quilting on Sunday afternoons during the
summer.

Location: Fourth St. and Indiana on the campus of Texas Tech
University

Hours: Tuesday - Sunday 10:00 a.m. - 5:00 p.m.

Admission: FREE

SCIENCE SPECTRUM/OMNIMAX THEATER
806-745-2525

This hands-on science, nature, and technology museum is especially for kids. Over seventy exhibits, films, and demonstrations
let you learn through discovery. You can make a giant bubble,
wonder at a spiral tornado, launch a hot air balloon, or even pre-
tend you're a jet pilot. "Kidspace" is a special area for
preschoolers.

Location: 2579 S. Loop 289

Museum hours: Monday - Saturday 10:00 a.m. - 5:30 p.m., Sunday 1:00 - 8:00 p.m.

Admission: $5.50/adults, $4.50/seniors 60+ and children 3-16

OMNIMAX AT THE SCIENCE SPECTRUM

806-745-6299

This theater uses the largest film frame in cinematic history (70 mm.) and advanced projectors to project images on a huge 58-ft diameter dome screen, visually surrounding the audience.

Omnimax hours: Monday - Thursday 11:00 a.m. - 8:00 p.m., Friday and Saturday 11:00 a.m. - 10:00 p.m., Sunday 1:00 - 8:00 p.m.

Admission: $5.75/adults, $4.50/seniors 60+ and children 3-16

TEXAS WATER RAMPAGE

806-796-0701

Cool off in this water theme park—swim, splash, tube, and slide.

Location: On U.S. 62/82 one and a half miles west of Loop 289

Hours: Summer: daily noon - 7:00 p.m.; opens at 11:00 a.m. on Saturdays

Admission: $12.75/adults; $6.75/juniors (under 4 feet tall), seniors, spectators, and after 4:00 p.m.

OTHER:

Brunswick South Plains Bowl - Cosmic Bowling - 5150 69th Street - 806-794-4844

Discovery Zone - 5025 50th Street - 806-792-5437

Grand Slam USA - 4620 71st Street - 806-784-0007

Jolly Time Arcade & Game Room - 6002 Slide Road, South Plains Mall - 806-799-1603

LaserPort - 5025 50th Street - 806-799-5689

Lubbock Crickets - baseball - 806-749-BALL

Putt-Putt Golf and Games - 5110 29th Drive - 806-795-2312

The Rink - Ice Skating, Roller Skating - 81st and Oakridge - 806-798-1361

Skate Ranch - 4701 SW Loop 289 - 806-792-0456

Southwest Sportsplex Ice Skating - 7116 82nd Street - 806-798-8442

McLean

Devil's Rope Museum

806-779-2225

See a huge collection of barbed wire artifacts, including displays of maps and photos of such famous area ranches as the 6666, XIT, JA, RO, and Frying Pan. The museum also displays a collection of U.S. Route 66 memorabilia including re-creations of the old "66" cafe and a tourist court. Handicapped accessible.

Location: Kingsley St. and old U.S. 66

Hours: April - October: Tuesday - Saturday 10:00 a.m. - 4:00 p.m., Sunday 1:00 p.m. - 4:00 p.m.

MULESHOE

NATIONAL MULE MEMORIAL

Taking your picture with this mule is much easier than the more lively kind. This unique monument pays tribute to the mules that pulled the covered wagons westward, plowed the sod for pioneers, and helped build the first railroads and highways. Mule Day is celebrated Labor Day weekend. Ever see a mule rodeo? Or mule races?

Location: Near the intersection of U.S. 70/84 downtown

MULESHOE NATIONAL WILDLIFE REFUGE

806-946-3341

Don't overlook the prairie dog colony along the entrance road. This is the oldest National Wildlife Refuge in Texas, founded in 1935. You'll see mostly migratory waterfowl; the largest concentration of sandhill cranes in the nation winters here.

Location: About 20 miles south on Texas 214

Hours: Open daylight hours

PANHANDLE

CARSON COUNTY SQUARE HOUSE MUSEUM

806-537-3524

Designed to be child-friendly, this is really one of the nicest small museums in the state. As soon as you enter this town, you'll see the Square House Museum complex, with indoor and outdoor exhibits interpreting the history and art of the Texas

Panhandle. Several period buildings, outbuildings, and structures have been meticulously restored. A Santa Fe caboose, set on track, contains early railroad memorabilia. The historic Square House, dating from the mid-1880s, is listed in the National Register.

Location: Fifth St. and Elsie (Pioneer Park)

Hours: Monday - Friday 9:00 a.m. - 5:00 p.m., Saturday 9:00 a.m. - 5:30 p.m., Sunday 1:00 - 5:30 p.m.

Admission: FREE

PLAINVIEW

Chamber of Commerce
806-296-7431
http://www.texasonline.net/chamber/

KIDSVILLE

Kids love Kidsville! This is a great park featuring state-of-the-art playground equipment and 10,000 square feet of safe family fun entertainment.

Location: Fourth St. and Ennis in Running Water Park

LLANO ESTACADO MUSEUM

Now known as the home of the "Easter Elephant," this was once just another nice museum with artifacts, gems and minerals, and re-created pioneer rooms. A remarkable discovery in May 1988 changed all that. The remains of the prehistoric Imperial Mammoth, elephant skull and tusks, discovered near the community of Easter, became known as "Easter Elephant" and was moved to its new home in the museum.

Location: 1900 W. Eighth (Wayland Baptist University campus)

Hours: Weekdays 9:00 a.m. - 5:00 p.m.; weekends March -
November: 1:00 p.m. - 5:00 p.m.

QUITAQUE

(Kit-a-Kway)
Quitaque Chamber of Commerce
806-455-1456

CAPROCK CANYONS STATE PARK

806-455-1492
http://www.tpwd.state.tx.us/park/parks.htm

Is that a bison? See pronghorn sheep, mule deer, white-tailed
deer, coyotes, bobcats, and even an occasional golden eagle in
this 14,000-acre state park. Erosion has carved spectacular landscapes at the edge of the Cap Rock. Most visitors are startled to
see such colorful cliffs and canyons and abundant wildlife in this
surprisingly scenic region of Texas.

Hikers and backpackers can enjoy 90 miles of trails within the
park. Facilities include covered picnic areas with grills, large
campgrounds with electricity, water, and covered tables at each
hook-up, two primitive camping areas, and an equestrian camping area with individual corrals and water for your horses. In
addition, you'll find equestrian trails, over 14 miles of well-
marked nature trails, exhibits, an amphitheater, a scenic drive,
and guided tours. At the 120-acre Lake Theo, there's swimming,
a beach area, fishing pier, and boat ramp.

Location: Park entrance is from the south on Ranch Road 1065

SHAMROCK

Appropriate to this town's ethnic orientation, shamrocks are embedded in the sidewalks and a genuine piece of the Blarney Stone from ruins of Blarney Castle, County Cork, Ireland, is displayed in Elmore Park. Shamrock is also located on Old Route 66.

> The water tower in downtown Shamrock looms at 190 feet tall and is considered the tallest in the state of Texas.

PIONEER WEST MUSEUM

Another small town museum, housed in the former Reynolds Hotel, this is full of exhibits with an emphasis on regional history, cowboys, farm and ranch artifacts, and pioneer weapons. Room settings include vintage doctor and dentist offices, general store, schoolroom, and pioneer kitchen.

Location: 204 N. Madden St.

Hours: Monday - Friday 10:00 a.m. - noon, 1:00 - 3:00 p.m.

West Texas

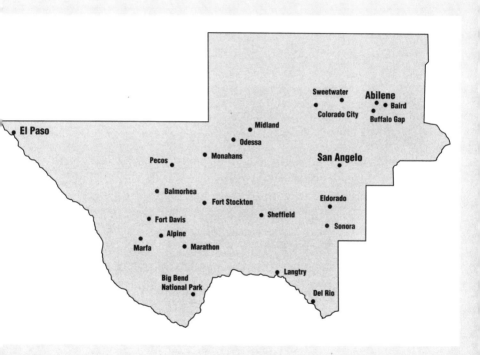

Sweetwater

Abilene
Baird

Colorado City

Buffalo Gap

El Paso

Midland

Odessa

Monahans

Pecos

San Angelo

Balmorhea

Fort Stockton

Eldorado

Fort Davis

Sheffield

Sonora

Alpine

Marfa

Marathon

Langtry

Big Bend
National Park

Del Rio

ABILENE

Convention & Visitors Bureau
Housed in the restored historic 1910 T&P Railroad Depot
1101 North First (at Cypress St.)
800-727-7704 or 915-676-2556
http://www.abilene.com/visitors/

Abilene was named for Abilene, Kansas, the end of the old Chisolm Trail. It has deep roots in the heritage of the Old West yet offers all the exciting benefits and activities of a thriving modern city.

ABILENE STATE PARK

915-572-3204
http://www.tpwd.state.tx.us

See part of the official Texas longhorn herd! This 621-acre park is set on brushy prairie land, with wooded valleys containing streams and groves of juniper, mesquite, cedar, native pecan, live oaks, red oaks, and hackberry. Large groves of native pecan trees used to attract Indians long before the arrival of Easterners in the area. Excellent facilities include a variety of campsites and RV accommodations found in four separate campgrounds.

Park activities include sand volleyball, horseshoes, children's wading pool, and swimming. Buffalo Wallow Pond offers great fishing, and hiking trails wander beside the creeks. View such wildlife as white-tailed deer, raccoons, armadillos, foxes, squirrels, cottontail rabbits, and a sizable variety of birds.

Location: About 16 miles southwest of town, south on FM 89, through Buffalo Gap, then on Park Road 32 to the park entrance

ABILENE ZOO AND DISCOVERY CENTER

915-676-6085

http://camalott.com/abilene/zoo/

Kids of all ages enjoy the Abilene Zoo, one of the five largest in Texas. Abilene's top visitor attraction covers thirteen acres and exhibits more than five hundred species of birds, mammals, reptiles, amphibians, and invertebrates. The Discovery Center is a climate-controlled series of indoor habitats including aquariums, a tropical aviary, and the Terrestrial Trail, which exhibits mongooses, lemurs, and ringtails.

Adjacent Nelson Park offers picnic areas, a playground, and soft-ball fields. Piddle Paddle (695-8747) in Nelson Park rents paddleboats weekends and holidays noon to dusk.

Location: About three miles east on Texas 36 at Loop 322

Hours: Memorial Day - Labor Day: Monday - Friday 9:00 a.m. - 5 p.m., weekends and holidays from 9:00 a.m. - 7:00 p.m.; Labor Day - Memorial Day: daily 9:00 a.m. - 5:00 p.m.; closed New Year's Day, Thanksgiving, and Christmas

Admission: $3/adults, $2/seniors and children ages 3-12

BUFFALO GAP HISTORIC VILLAGE—see: BUFFALO GAP

CHILDREN'S MUSEUM

915-673-4587

Excitement and education meet as children of all ages enjoy interactive and hands-on learning exhibits such as Kidsville, KIDD-TV, and computers. Laugh and learn in the Fifties diner, video art room, echo tunnel, and other areas. The Children's Museum is part of a complex of three museums in the Grace

 **West Texas** ABILENE

Cultural Center, located in the historic Grace Hotel across from the historic Texas and Pacific Depot. The other two are the Abilene Historical Museum and the Fine Arts Museum.

Location: 102 Cypress Street

Hours: Tuesday, Wednesday, Friday, and Saturday from 10:00 a.m. to 5:00 p.m., Thursdays from 10:00 a.m. to 8:30 p.m.

Admission: $2/adults, $1/children 12 and under, FREE on Thursdays from 5:00 p.m. to 8:30 p.m.

DYESS AIR FORCE BASE/LINEAR AIR PARK
915-696-5609

If you like airplanes, go out to Dyess AFB. Thirty aircraft from WW II to the present are displayed along the main base thoroughfare. Dyess Air Force Base is a large military base, the sole training base for crews of the B-1 bomber, and home to an air combat command wing. There's no entrance fee, but you'll have to stop at the main gate for a temporary pass.

FORT PHANTOM HILL

Another small piece of Texas history is found north of town—an old army post, established in 1851 to protect the frontier from Indians. All you can see now are the ruins of three buildings and several chimneys.

Location: From I-20, drive north on FM 600 for 14 miles or take the Texas Forts Trail route on FM 2833.

Hours: Open daily

Admission: FREE

28

PARAMOUNT THEATER

915-676-9620

This is probably a more nostalgic trip for adults, but if the kids haven't seen a theater other than the modern multi-unit ones, this is a must. The Paramount is on the National Register of Historic Places and has been restored to the grandeur of yesteryear. Inside the magnificent Art Deco building, you'll find drifting clouds and twinkling stars on a blue sky, neon and incandescent cove lighting, and domed turrets. Classic films, plays, and concerts are presented throughout the year.

Location: 352 Cypress

Hours: Open for self-guided tours weekdays from 1:00 p.m. - 5:00 p.m.

OTHER:

Abilene Speedway - car racing (dirt track) - 6825 W. Business 20 - 692-8800

Abilene Fun Track - go-carts - 5549 S. First - 695-4634

Double J Horse Ranch - horseback riding - 6950 West Lake Rd. - 675-0945

Play Faire Park - miniature golf - 2300 N. Second - 672-2977

Putt Putt - miniature golf - 201 S. Danville - 692-7596

Family Roller Rink - roller skating - 201 Shelton - 676-8437

The Skatin' Place - roller skating - 1930 S. Clack - 695-4713

ALPINE

Alpine Chamber of Commerce
106 N. Third Street
800-561-3735 or 915-837-2326
http://www.alpinetexas.com

This small town is the gateway to Big Bend Country. One route, Texas 118, leads in a southerly direction to the western entrance of Big Bend National Park near Terlingua and Study Butte. The other main route to the park, U.S. 385, lies to the east of Alpine, leading south from U.S. Highway 90, thirty-one miles east of town. Park roads connect the two main routes, providing a scenic loop drive to and from Alpine. The Texas Cowboy Poetry Gathering in early March draws thousands of visitors from around the country. The hot air balloon festival over Labor Day is also worth putting on your schedule.

APACHE TRADING POST

915-837-5506

This is an interesting shop with rocks, fossils, minerals, and numerous Big Bend collectibles and a huge collection of maps of the Big Bend region.

Location: About three miles west of town on U.S. 90

Hours: Monday - Saturday 9:00 a.m. - 6:00 p.m., Sunday 1:00 p.m. - 6:00 p.m.

MUSEUM OF THE BIG BEND

915-837-8143
http://www.sulross.edu/~museum/

This outstanding museum showcases the history of the Big Bend area with displays, dioramas, and paintings.

30

Location: Sul Ross State University campus

Hours: Tuesday - Saturday 9:00 a.m. - 5:00 p.m., Sunday 1:00 p.m. - 5:00 p.m.

Admission: FREE

> Armadillos have four young, always of the same sex, which are identical quadruplets developed from the same egg.

WOODWARD AGATE RANCH

915-364-2271

Are you a rock hound? Here you can hunt and collect various types of agate, colorful jasper, labradorite feldspar, calcite, precious opal, and other minerals on over 3,000 acres. You can buy what you find, and ranch experts will help grade it. There's also a lapidary shop.

Location: About 18 miles south of Alpine on Texas 118

BAIRD

Chamber of Commerce
100 Market
915-854-2003
http://bairdtexas.com/

GRUMPE'S SPECIALTIES

915-854-1106

Lollipops galore! Grumpe's is a manufacturer of suckers and a fascinating place to tour. It's a wholesale business that makes promotional suckers for clients in every state in the U.S. and five foreign countries. Currently located on the main street of Baird, a tour through the facility can be arranged by calling in

advance. However, the company is planning an expansion and relocation to a site along the interstate highway in 1999 that will have a retail storefront and expanded touring capabilities and the appearance of a "candy factory."

BALMORHEA

Balmorhea Chamber of Commerce
915-375-2272

BALMORHEA STATE PARK

915-389-8900
http://www.tpwd.state.tx.us

This is the place to go swimming! A huge walled swimming pool is fed by the springs at the rate of 22 to 26 million gallons a day. At 62,000 square feet, it's one of the largest man-made pools in the U.S. Camping and motel facilities are available.

> Balmorhea State Park claims the world's largest spring-fed swimming pool.

Scuba dive in San Solomon Springs! Here you'll find the best freshwater diving in Texas. The crystal clear waters are approximately 28 feet deep and maintain an average water temperature of 74 degrees. Dive and swim year round. Scuba lessons and supplies are available.

Location: Four miles west on Texas 17

Hours: Open all year

BIG BEND NATIONAL PARK

915-477-2251
http://www.nps.gov/bibe/

 Dozens of books have been written about this area of magnificent contrasts! Truly an outstanding collection of ecosystems, it's a geological showplace, sprawling over 800,000 acres. It is a vast land that invites exploring, not a park that can be seen in just a few hours.

Big Bend is one of America's great national parks, still largely unknown to non-Texans, but gaining popularity among nature lovers who come here to gaze upon the stark landscape and enjoy the wild beauty of the Chihuahuan Desert. The variation in elevation and temperature makes Big Bend an ideal year-round park.

 A hundred million years ago, this area was ocean. Sixty-five million years ago, dinosaurs roamed the area, along with other ancient creatures, such as the Big Bend Pterodactyl, the largest flying creature known, with an estimated 51-foot wingspread.

You'll see an incredible diversity of plants (more than 1,200 types), over 450 species of birds, and animal life just as varied. Rangers present walks and illustrated talks throughout the year.

Explore more than 150 miles of trails, 100 miles of paved roads, and 170 miles of dirt roads. Permits are required for all back-country and primitive camping, also for all river users. Free permits may be obtained at park visitor centers. Pets are not permitted on any trail or outside developed areas and must be kept on a leash at all times in developed areas.

The main visitor center is in the middle of the park at Panther Junction at the intersection of U.S. 385 and Texas 118. Basic

facilities in the park include National Park Service campgrounds, a trailer park, store/gas station, post office, and lodge/gift shop/restaurant in the Chisos Mountain Basin.

Visitor centers throughout the park offer information, maps, and exhibits. Panther Junction is open year round 8:00 a.m. - 6:00 p.m.; the ones in Chisos Basin, Persimmon Gap, and Rio Grande Village are open seasonally.

For information or to make reservations, write National Park Concessions Inc., Big Bend National Park, TX 79834-9999 or call 915-477-2291.

Several licensed outfitters provide river rafting or float trips and wilderness excursions. An approved list may be obtained from the park.

Companies offering guided float trips are:

- Big Bend River Tours, Lajitas; 915-424-3219 or 800-545-4240
- Far Flung Adventures, Terlingua; 915-371-2489 or 800-359-4138
- Texas River Expeditions, Terlingua; 915-371-2633 or 800-839-7238

Equipment rentals are available from:

- Ivey Enterprises (rafts), Terlingua; 915-371-2424
- Scott Shuttle Service (canoes), Marathon; 915-386-4574

BUFFALO GAP

BUFFALO GAP HISTORIC VILLAGE

915-572-3365
http://www.abilene.com/art/bgap/

This is a great place to learn about the tumultuous history of the area. The village consists of twenty authentic buildings, mostly over one hundred years old. The original Taylor County courthouse and jail now houses western and Indian artifacts from the area. The oldest structure is a log cabin; others include the train station, church, doctor's office, cabinet mill, blacksmith shop, barber shop, print shop, wagon barn, "filling" station, art gallery, school, bank, post office, and the Buffalo Gap Store and Trading Post. The home of the first marshal of Abilene has now been restored with most of its original contents.

Location: About 14 miles south of Abilene; take FM 89 to Buffalo Gap, turn right on Elm for two blocks.

Hours: Summer (March 15 - November 15): Monday - Saturday 10:00 a.m. - 6:00 p.m., Sunday noon - 6:00 p.m.; winter (November 16 - March 14): Friday & Saturday 10:00 a.m. - 4:00 p.m., Sunday noon - 5:00 p.m.; closed Thanksgiving and Christmas

Admission: $4/adults, $3/seniors 65+, $1.75/students grades 1-12, under 6 free

PERINI RANCH STEAKHOUSE

915-572-3339

Since Texas is cattle country, you'll find steaks on almost every restaurant menu. For tender, well-aged steaks, try the Perini Ranch Steakhouse, located on the Perini Ranch in

Buffalo Gap. The restaurant also serves burgers, barbecue, and other grilled foods.

Location: Wednesday and Thursday for dinner, Friday - Sunday for lunch and dinner

COLORADO CITY

Chamber of Commerce
915-728-3403
http://www.bitstreet.com/ccity/index.html

THE BRANDING WALL

What a wall! They call it the Branding Wall—over 230 cattle brands used in Mitchell County are displayed on a 10' x 50' wall, signifying the importance of ranching to the area.

Location: Second and Chestnut St. downtown in Kiwanis Park

 ### LAKE COLORADO CITY STATE PARK
915/728-3931
http://www.tpwd.state.tx.us/park/parks.htm

This 500-acre park offers more than five miles of shoreline for swimming, fishing, camping, hiking, and picnicking. Visitors of all ages enjoy seeing part of the Texas longhorn herd here. Facilities include restrooms with showers, picnic tables with grills, campsites and pull-through RV sites, trailer dump stations, boat ramp, lighted pier, and a Texas State Park store.

Location: About 11 miles southwest of Colorado City off I-20 on FM 2836

DEL RIO

Del Rio Camber of Commerce
1915 Ave. F
830-775-3551
http://www.chamber.delrio.com/

Enjoy a "two-nation vacation"—local transportation makes it easy to visit Ciudad Acuña just across the Mexican border. If you are an American citizen, you don't need a passport as long as you don't travel farther than a border town or stay longer than 72 hours. But carry proof of citizenship with you to re-enter the U.S.

LAKE AMISTAD RECREATION AREA

http://www.nps.gov/amis/

The huge international Amistad Reservoir offers free campgrounds, swimming beaches, marinas, and boat ramps on the U.S. side. The lake is surrounded by dramatic limestone cliffs and caves, many of which are accessible only by boat; one of these, Panther Cave, contains Indian pictographs. Get maps and information at the headquarters on U.S. 90 at the western edge of Del Rio.

VAL VERDE WINERY

One of the most historic sites in Del Rio, this family enterprise was founded in 1883 by Italian immigrants. Still operated by the family, now the fourth generation, the winery welcomes visitors.

Hours: Monday - Saturday 9:00 a.m. - 5:00 p.m.

EL PASO

Convention & Visitors Bureau
1 Civic Center Plaza
800-351-6024 or 915-534-0600
http://www.elpasocvb.com/

El Paso ("the pass") sprawls from its origin in an ancient mountain pass in the Franklin Mountains. You'll find a quiet village of great charm and historic color, with thick-walled adobe buildings clustered around the old church and Spanish plaza as they were one hundred years ago.

ASCARATE PARK—see also: WESTERN PLAYLAND AMUSEMENT PARK

915-772-3914

This 440-acre facility has a 44-acre man-made lake stocked with catfish, bass, and trout; eight softball diamonds; a baseball field; a golf course; an aquatic center with Olympic-sized 50-meter pool; and is home to Western Playland amusement park.

Location: Six miles east of town; take I-10 to the Trowbridge exit, go south to Delta, turn right and go over the bridge, then left into Ascarate Park.

BORDER PATROL MUSEUM

915-759-6060

The movies have portrayed the border patrol in various lights, but here you can learn the real history of the U.S. Border Patrol from the Old West to the present. Displays show surveillance equipment, confiscated items, aircraft and vehicles used by the patrol, and more. This 10,000-square-foot museum makes a good stop, as does the Wilderness Park Museum next door.

Location: 4315 Transmountain Road

Hours: Monday - Friday 9:00 a.m. - 5:00 p.m.

El Paso Saddle Blanket Trading Post
915-544-1000

This unique store has been an El Paso landmark for twenty-five years. Shop for blankets, rugs, Indian artifacts, and Mexican imports.

Location: 601 N. Oregon

El Paso Zoo
915-544-1928

Newly expanded and improved, the El Paso Zoo is the major zoo in the entire west Texas, southern New Mexico, and northern Mexico region. It's home to over seven hundred animals, including many endangered species, which live in eighteen acres of natural habitat. Visitors may enter the 8,000-square foot aviary and observe exotic birds up close.

Location: Near the intersection of Highway 54 and Paisano

Hours: Daily 9:30 a.m. - 4:00 p.m.

Admission: $3/ages 12-61, $1.50/ages 3-11 and 62+, 2 and under free

Insights—El Paso Science Center
915-534-0000

Exhibits here are designed to make learning about science and technology an active experience. The center features hands-on exhibits about science and technology: solar power, motion,

light, illumination, electricity, space science, computers, energy, and the human body.

Location: 505 N. Santa Fe St.

Hours: Tuesday - Saturday 9:00 a.m. - 5:00 p.m.; closed major holidays

Admission: $5/adults, $4/military and students, $3/children and sentiors

SCENIC DRIVE

 Take an extraordinarily scenic drive along the Trans-Mountain Road (Loop 375) through the mountains. An aerial tramway ascends Ranger Peak for a 360-degree view of three states and two nations and the Rio Grande!

TIGUA INDIAN RESERVATION

915-859-7913

Experience another culture! Established in 1681, this is the oldest community within the present boundaries of Texas. Ysleta del Sur Pueblo Cultural Center is owned and operated by the Tigua Indians. Visit the museum and gift shop, see arts and crafts demonstrations and Indian social dancing, eat fresh Indian bread at the Cacique Cafe.

Location: 305 Yaya Lane

Hours: Tuesday - Friday 9:00 a.m. - 4:00 p.m., Saturday - Sunday 9:00 a.m. - 5:00 p.m.

WESTERN PLAYLAND AMUSEMENT PARK—see also: ASCARATE PARK

915-772-3914
www.WesternPlayland.com

This 25-acre amusement park features dozens of rides for all ages—roller coasters, water slides, trains, go-carts, and more in a well-maintained and exceptionally clean park. The park also has entertainment pavilions, picnic areas, games, shops, and food. This is a great place to let the kids unwind after too much time in the car.

Location: In Ascarate Park, six miles east of El Paso; exit I-10 at Trowbridge and turn south, turn right on Delta and go over the bridge, then left into the park.

Hours: Weekends in the spring and fall and Wednesday - Sunday in the summer

Admission: Pay One Price (P.O.P.) $13.50 (excluding go-carts)

WET 'N' WILD WATERWORLD

915-886-2222
www.wetwild.com

Thirty-seven acres of good, clean, family fun—this well-established waterpark just keeps getting bigger and better. Dozens of water attractions for everyone including the new "Screamer," a six-story-tall water slide that goes almost straight down. With huge shade trees and picnic areas, this is a great place to beat the El Paso heat.

Location: In Anthony, Texas (Exit 0 off I-10), about 17 miles west of downtown.

Hours: Vary; extended in summer

Admission: $16/adults, $14/children 4-12, children 3 and under free, $11/non-swimmers

CATTLEMAN'S STEAKHOUSE AT INDIAN CLIFFS RANCH

915-544-3200
http://www.CattlemansSteakhouse.com

 The whole family will have fun at this twenty-six-year-old landmark east of El Paso. You can see Texas longhorns, buffalo, deer, Belgian team horses, and many other animals. There's also an Indian maze, movie set, the Fort Apache playground for kids, and hayrides on Sunday afternoons. Admission is FREE for steakhouse guests. So stay for dinner at the world-famous Cattleman's Steakhouse.

Location: 35 miles from downtown; take I-10 east to exit 49, north about five miles

Hours: Open daily for dinner and for lunch and dinner on Sundays.

OTHER:

 El Paso Speedway - stock cars and dragsters

Champions Sportsplex - outdoor recreational facilities - 915-857-7676

El Paso Diablos - professional baseball - 915-755-2000

El Paso Patriots - professional soccer - 915-771-6620

Putt-Putt Golf and Games - 915-779-2226

The Husdpeth County Courthouse in Sierra Blanca is the Southwest's only in-use government structure of adobe. It's a popular snapshot subject.

ELDORADO

X BAR RANCH

888-853-2688 or 915-853-2688
http://www.XbarRanch.com

Ever stay on a real working ranch? Here's your chance! The X Bar Ranch is tucked away in the rolling hills of Southwest Texas. On more than 7,000 acres, this working ranch offers guests the opportunity to experience real ranch life, enjoy nature at its absolute best, and taste the history and culture of this land. There are different accommodations to choose from, but all include breakfast, participation in ranch activities, access to hiking and mountain biking trails, nature trail system, birding, stock tank swimming, horseshoe pitching, observing ranch animals and wildlife, star gazing, and just relaxing.

X Bar Ranch
Photo courtesy of X Bar Ranch

And if that isn't enough, for an additional fee, you can saddle up and ride into the sunset or arrange chuckwagon dinners with entertainment. X Bar Ranch can be a base for the exploration of numerous attractions in the area. When you call for information, you'll get a list of activities and current events.

NATURAL WOOL OF TEXAS

915-853-2541
http://www.brackettville.com/eldoradowoolen/aboutus.htm

Wool in Texas? The Eldorado Woolen Mill is the first and oldest woolen mill in the Lone Star State. The mill is now owned by the townspeople of Eldorado and leased to a private business for production of various wool and mohair products. Lovely creations are made by skilled textile artisans.

Location: 409 S.W. Main St.

Hours: Monday - Friday 8:00 a.m. - 5:00 p.m., and Saturday 8:00 a.m. - 4:00 p.m. Tours may be arranged.

FORT DAVIS

Fort Davis Chamber of Commerce
800-524-3015 or 915-426-3015
http://www.fortdavis.com

This little town is full of character! Much of its early frontier atmosphere has been preserved with a number of original buildings and the longest remaining stretch of the famous Overland Trail. The town has a charming town square surrounded by buildings that date from the early 1900s. The Davis Mountains provide plenty of recreational activities for outdoor lovers.

Chihuahuan Desert Visitor Center

915-837-8370

Located in the rolling foothills of the Davis Mountains, this 500-acre tract is a living desert museum. Mainly a long-term research facility, it offers public seminars during the summer months on a wide variety of nature-related topics. Call for current schedules.

Location: Four miles south on Texas 118

Davis Mountains State Park

915-426-3337
http://www.tdpw.state.tx.us/park/parks.htm

The 2,700-acre Davis Mountains State Park is the focus of outdoor recreation in the Fort Davis area. It's certainly one of the most scenic parks in Texas with an elevation change of 1,000 feet. Don't miss Skyline Drive, a paved road that climbs steeply on the eastern side of the park to two overlook areas where you can see the roads to Alpine and Marfa, parts of Fort Davis, and Limpia Creek far below. Bird life is abundant, especially during spring and fall migrations. Several miles of hiking trails pass through oak, pinon, and juniper and lead to a canyon formed by Keesey Creek. Lodging is available at Indian Lodge (915-426-3254), a pueblo-style adobe hotel built by the CCC in the 1930s. If you're too young to remember the CCC, take time to find out about this part of our history. The park also offers a variety of camping, from RV hookups to primitive campsites.

Location: Four miles north of town via Texas 118

Admission: Camping and entrance fees vary

FORT DAVIS NATIONAL HISTORIC SITE

915-426-3224
http://www.nps.gov/foda/

Established in 1854, this was the first military post to guard the route between San Antonio and El Paso. After the Civil War, it was home to the "Buffalo Soldiers," many of them former slaves from Southern plantations. It's an excellent example of frontier forts from that era. During the summer, park rangers and volunteers (dressed as soldiers, officers' wives, and servants) provide information and answer questions in some of the buildings. The Visitor Center is in a restored barracks, along with a museum, bookstore, audio programs, and slide shows.

> Indians named the black soldiers "Buffalo Soldiers" out of respect for their skill and bravery.

Hours: Daily 8:00 a.m. - 5:00 p.m. (8:00 a.m. - 6:00 p.m. Memorial Day - Labor Day); closed national holidays. Operated by the National Park Service.

McDONALD OBSERVATORY

915-426-3640
http://www.as.utexas.edu/mcdonald/vc/default.html

Fascinating fun for everyone! Participate in guided or self-guided tours, solar viewing, star parties, and special events. Once a month visitors can look through the giant 107-inch telescope by making reservations with the Visitor Center. This event is very popular and sometimes booked months in advance.

The magnificent site, atop the 6,791-foot peak of Mount Locke, was selected because of the clear air, high number of cloudless nights, and distance from a large concentration of artificial lights.

Astronomy exhibits and a short orientation video are featured at the outstanding Visitor Center. The staff is available to answer questions, and its unique gift shop features astronomy-related items, unusual T-shirts, and lots of books.

Location: At the foot of Mount Locke, about 16 miles northwest of town on Texas 118

Hours: Daily 9:00 a.m. - 5:00 p.m.; closed New Year's Day, Thanksgiving, and Christmas

NEILL DOLL MUSEUM

915-426-3969 or 915-426-3838

This extensive collection of antique dolls, furniture, and buggies is displayed in the 1898 historic Trueheart home.

Location: Seven blocks west of the courthouse

Hours: Call for hours

"THE DRUGSTORE"

This really cool, old-fashioned soda fountain still serves malts, floats, and chocolate sodas. Who remembers lime phosphates? You can get burgers and sandwiches, too, and some say it serves the best breakfasts in the area. A jukebox plays fabulous Fifties music. A gift shop features western souvenirs. Located on Main Street.

> The longest undisturbed stretch of the Texas Overland Trail (San Antonio-El Paso Road) is in Fort Davis.

HOTEL LIMPIA

800-662-5517 or 915-426-3237
http://www.hotellimpia.com

It's easy to step back in history in this tiny town. The Hotel Limpia is much as it was when judges, doctors, and politicians came to Fort Davis to escape the sultry summers to the south and east. Built in 1912 of pink limestone, it retains its original pioneer character. Rocking chairs and wicker furniture fill expansive porches and a glassed-in veranda. The hotel's dining room is the best place in town to eat, too.

Location: Main Street on the square

PRUDE GUEST RANCH

800-458-6232 or 915-426-3202
http://pecos.net/news/pages/prude.htm

Prude Ranch is really a working ranch. It was established in 1898 as a cattle ranch. Today it's one of the few places left in the Southwest where visitors can enjoy the free feeling of wide-open spaces, lofty mountains, clean air, and pleasant temperatures. Facilities include a heated indoor swimming pool, lighted tennis courts, weight room, hydrotherapy spas, mountain trails for hiking, exercise room, TV and lounge area, and horseback riding. Various accommodations and RV hook-ups and campsites are available. Mealtime is a special treat with Cowboy breakfasts and Chuckwagon feasts.

Location: In the Davis Mountains, approximately six miles west of Fort Davis

Fort Stockton

Fort Stockton Tourism Division
800-334-8525
"The Caboose" Visitor Information Center
I-10 and U.S. 285
915-336-8052

Historic Fort Stockton

915-336-2400

Four original buildings remain; others have been reconstructed of this typical frontier military post. The fort originally consisted of thirty-five buildings made of adobe and hand-hewn limestone.

Location: 300 E. Third

Hours: Daily 10:00 a.m. - 5:00 p.m.

Admission: $1/adults, 50¢/children

Annie Riggs Memorial Museum

915-336-2167

Delightful reminders of the past, exhibits of yesteryear in Pecos County are housed in a 1900 Victorian adobe hotel. Every other Thursday night in the summer, free outdoor folk music concerts are held at the museum.

Location: 301 S. Main St.

Hours: Daily 10:00 a.m. - 5:00 p.m.

Admission: $1/adults, 50¢/children

PAISANO PETE

Pete is probably the world's largest roadrunner at 22 feet long and 11 feet tall. Take your picture with Pete to show the folks back home.

Location: U.S. 290 and Main Street

Paisano Pete
Photo courtesy of City of Fort Stockton

Langtry

"I'm fining you $45 and a round of drinks for the jury, and that's my ruling!" This is said to have been a ruling by one of the most colorful characters in western history. Judge Roy Bean, the "Law West of the Pecos," ruled with his own brand of justice during the last decades of the nineteenth century. Most cases were decided in the combination courtroom and saloon called the "Jersey Lilly." Tales about the unconventional justice of the peace multiplied until he became a legend. He's gone now, but the legends still live and the Jersey Lilly stills stands in Langtry.

The modern Texas Travel Visitor Center welcomes travelers and preserves a page of the Lone Star State's colorful history, so that we can see where the legend grew.

Marathon

Gage Hotel

800-884-GAGE

You can easily step back in time here in this restored West Texas hotel of the 1920s. Comfortable guestrooms are available in the old hotel and the restored stables near the courtyard and pool. The restaurant serves excellent regional fare.

Location: On U.S. 90

MARFA

Marfa Chamber of Commerce
915-729-4942
http://www.marfalights.com

The Marfa Mystery Lights were first reported by early settlers in 1883. The mysterious lights, sometimes called "ghost lights," still defy explanation. The historical marker at the prime viewing area, nine miles east of the city on U.S. 90, gives details.

Marfa's other claim to fame is that the 1955 motion picture *Giant*, starring Rock Hudson, James Dean, and Elizabeth Taylor, was filmed here. The stars stayed in private houses while most of the other actors and crew stayed in the El Paisano Hotel, which still operates today.

Climb into the dome of the Presidio County Courthouse for a breathtaking panorama of the mountains surrounding Marfa. Marfa's 9-hole golf course is the highest golf course in Texas.

MIDLAND

Convention & Visitors Bureau
109 N. Main
800-624-6435 or 915-683-3381

CONFEDERATE AIR FORCE AND AMERICAN AIRPOWER HERITAGE MUSEUM

915-563-1000
www.avdigest.com/caf/caf.html
www.avdigest.com/aahm/aahm.html

Are you a vintage airplane buff? Then see the nation's finest and most complete collection of flyable WW II combat aircraft. This museum is dedicated to the acquisition, restoration, and preservation (in flying condition) of vintage military aircraft of the United States, Britain, Germany, and Japan. "Airsho" each October draws thousands of spectators.

Location: Midland International Airport

Hours: Monday - Saturday 9:00 a.m. - 5:00 p.m., Sundays and holidays 12:00 noon - 5:00 p.m.; closed Thanksgiving and Christmas

PARKS

Midland has an extensive park system throughout the city. Dennis the Menace Park is three acres of colorful wading pools, walks, slides, playhouses, and fountains. Hogan Park has picnic areas, playgrounds, a swimming pool, ball diamonds, a 27-hole golf course, and the Sibley Nature Center and Trail. Chris Davidson Memorial Park is one of only three parks in the U.S. that is totally accessible for wheelchairs. It offers a merry-go-round, swings, physical fitness courses, basketball and volleyball courts, and a gazebo.

PERMIAN BASIN PETROLEUM MUSEUM AND HALL OF FAME

915-683-4403

Walk "under" a vast sea, viewing the Permian Basin as it was 230 million years ago! Stroll down the sidewalk of a bustling "boomtown" of the last century. Explore the geology that created oil rich West Texas. Learn how wells are drilled. Experience the intense heat and frightful sound of a well gone wild. Try your luck in the "Oil Game." A fun-filled learning experience! This is an outstanding museum for visitors of all ages.

Location: I-20 West at exit 136

Hours: Monday - Saturday 9:00 a.m. - 5:00 p.m., Sunday 2:00 - 5:00 p.m.; closed Thanksgiving, Christmas Eve, and Christmas Day

Admission: $3/adults, $2.50/seniors, $1.50/children under 12

FREDDA TURNER DURHAM CHILDREN'S MUSEUM

915-683-2882

This interactive museum encourages exploration with exhibits for children ages four to twelve, a computer area, and a preschool play area.

Location: 1705 W. Missouri Ave.

Hours: Tuesday - Saturday 10:00 a.m. - 5:00 p.m., Sunday 2:00 - 5:00 p.m.

Admission: FREE

OTHER:

Midland Angels - baseball - 915-683-4251

Midland Polo Club - professional polo season April - September - 915-684-6493

Putt Putt Golf and Games - 3415 Loop 250 West

MONAHANS

MONAHANS SANDHILLS STATE PARK
http://www/tpwd.state.tx.us/park/parks.htm

Four thousand acres of wind-sculptured sand dunes seem to appear from nowhere like the landscape of the Sahara Desert. You'll find a modern museum and interpretive center, picnicking, camping, and sand surfing at this unusual park.

Location: Five miles east at I-20 and U.S. 80

ODESSA

Convention & Visitors Bureau
700 North Grant, suite 200
1-800-780-HOST (4678)
http://www.tourtexas.com/odessa/odessa2do.html

Get your picture taken with the "World's Largest Jackrabbit," a 10-foot statue in the school administration's parking lot at 802 N. Sam Houston.

PRESIDENTIAL MUSEUM
915-322-7123

This unusual museum is the only one in the United States dedicated to the office of the presidency and all the men who have served from George Washington to the present. Campaign slogans, buttons, and posters (some of them bizarre) are displayed. A magnificent collection of dolls shows the hairstyles and inaugural gowns of every first lady. It took over twenty years to

research and craft the intricate miniature dresses. If you want to do some homework while you're there, the museum has a vast presidential research facility. A gift shop is located in the museum.

Location: 622 N. Lee

Hours: Tuesday - Saturday 10:00 a.m. - 5:00 p.m.; closed major holidays

Admission: $2

PECOS

Pecos Chamber of Commerce
111 South Cedar (Highway 285)
915-445-2406
http://www.texasusa.com/pecos

"The home of the world's first rodeo" is Pecos' claim to fame. Originated in 1883, one of the world's most famous rodeos is staged where it began each Fourth of July weekend.

 ### MAXEY PARK AND ZOO

"Kids City" recreation area attracts children of all ages with baseball/softball fields, basketball courts, and a miniature golf course. The park has a picnic area, gazebo, and botanical garden. A full facility campground and RV park is just west of the park. The zoo features several species of animals: buffalo, deer, javelina, cougars, zebra, and antelope.

Location: I-20 between U.S. 285 and Texas 17

WEST OF THE PECOS MUSEUM

This interesting museum occupies the old saloon and three floors of the historic hotel, once the area's finest. Renowned as one of the most complete collections of western memorabilia anywhere! See accurate displays of life in the late 1800s and the site where quick-draw bartender Barney Riggs gunned down two outlaws. The adjacent park contains the first building in Pecos; the grave of Clay Allison, the "Gentleman Gunfighter"; and a replica of Judge Roy Bean's saloon, the "Jersey Lilly." It also houses the tourist center offices.

Location: 120 E. First

Hours: Monday - Saturday 9:00 a.m. - 5:00 p.m., Sunday 2:00 - 5:00 p.m.

SAN ANGELO

Convention & Visitors Bureau
500 Rio Concho Dr. at Convention Center
800-375-1206 or 915-653-1206
http://www.sanangelo-tx.com

ANGELO STATE UNIVERSITY PLANETARIUM

915-942-2136
915-942-2188 for star date information

Get a three-dimensional view of the universe! Watch celestial fireworks and stars at the nation's fourth largest university planetarium. Located in the Nursing-Physical Science building on the Angelo State campus, the planetarium features twice-weekly programs for public viewing, except on holidays and semester breaks.

Location: Angelo State University campus

Hours: Shows are at 8:00 p.m. Thursdays and 2:00 p.m. Saturdays

Admission: $3/adults, $1.50/students, faculty, seniors, children

FORT CONCHO NATIONAL HISTORIC LANDMARK
915-481-2646

San Angelo literally grew up around Fort Concho; now the town boasts the fort as its primary tourist attraction. One of the best-preserved forts of the Texas frontier, this 40-acre National Historic Landmark is comprised of twenty-three original and restored buildings. Most stone structures were built with pecan-wood beams and rafters by skilled German craftsmen from Fredericksburg. Exhibits tell the story of the fort, the Indian campaigns, and San Angelo. Other excellent museums are in various buildings on the grounds, including the Museum of Telephony and the Museum of Frontier Medicine.

Location: 630 S. Oakes St.

Hours: Tuesday - Saturday 10:00 a.m. - 5:00 p.m., Sunday 1:00 - 5:00 p.m.; closed New Year's Day, Thanksgiving, and Christmas

RIVER WALK

The Concho River, named for the mussels that produce the unique pink Concho pearl, has always been a treasure to the city. The city can be proud of its efforts to beautify the downtown area. Along the 4.5-mile river walk are colorful gardens and huge pecan trees, a plaza area, waterfalls and fountains, turn-of-the-century lighting, a jogging-walking trail, a 9-hole golf course, a miniature golf course, a children's amusement park, and RiverStage.

- Neff's Amusement Park features rides for young and old. Open during the summer only; opens at 6:30 p.m. weekdays, and 1:30 p.m. Saturday and Sunday. 915-653-3014

- RiverStage showcases a broad spectrum of events including touring musicals, dance reviews, pop concerts, melodramas, band concerts, and the annual Cactus Jazz and Blues Festival in September. 915-657-4450 or 915-657-4290

SAN ANGELO CHILDREN'S ART MUSEUM

915-659-4391

A giant kaleidoscope, gravity well, fun mirror, facepaint station, and fun computer programs await young visitors in the Cactus Hotel. Kids will find hands-on activities to explore and create. The Cactus Hotel was Conrad Hilton's fourth hotel. Built in 1929, it was the largest, most ornate, and most expensive, at an extravagant cost of $900,000. The hotel, with its fourteen stories, lavish decorations, and elegant crystal ballroom, has been revitalized as the city's cultural center.

Location: 36 E. Twohig

Hours: Tuesday - Friday 1:00 - 5:00 p.m., Saturday 10:00 a.m. - 5:00 p.m., Sunday 1:00 - 5:00 p.m.

Admission: $2; FREE on Tuesdays

SAN ANGELO NATURE CENTER

915-942-0121

Especially for kids, this regional natural science museum features displays of native wildlife, a 200-gallon aquarium, a small collection of live animals, nature trails, and audiovisual programs.

Location: 7409 Knickerbocker Road (Mary Lee Park)

Hours: Summer: Wednesday - Sunday 10:00 a.m. - 4:00 p.m.; rest of the year: Tuesday - Saturday 1:00 - 6:00 p.m.

 ## SAN ANGELO STATE PARK
915-949-4757 or 915-947-2687
http://www.tpwd.state.tx.us/park/parks.htm

Boat, fish, swim, hike, mountain bike, horseback ride, and view wildlife in this 7,563-acre park. Interpretive guided tours are scheduled year round to explain the paleontology and archaeology found in the park—petroglyph tours, dinosaur walks, and stargazing parties.

Location: O.C. Fisher Reservoir along the western boundary of the city

OTHER:

 San Angelo Speedway - auto racing - 915-659-5172

Wall Dragway - 915-947-0588

College Hills Miniature Golf and Games - 915-949-6470

Texas Putting Courses - 915-653-1805

8-Wheels Skating Center - 915-942-8506

SHEFFIELD

FORT LANCASTER STATE HISTORIC SITE

http://www.tpwd.state.tx.us/park/parks.htm

Established in 1855 by the First U.S. Infantry. Troopers on mules protected wagon trains on the "lower road" between San Antonio and El Paso. A modern interpretive center welcomes visitors. Located on Hwy 290.

Hours: Daily Memorial Day - Labor Day: 9:00 a.m. - 6:00 p.m.;
rest of the year: Thursday - Monday 9:00 a.m. - 5:00 p.m.

SONORA

Chamber of Commerce
707 N. Crockett
915-387-2880

CAVERNS OF SONORA

915-387-3105

"This is the most indescribably beautiful cavern in the world. Its
beauty cannot be exaggerated, even by Texans!" This quote by
Bill Stephenson, founder of the National Speleological Society,
accurately describes the Caverns of Sonora. Formations
described as "impossible" grow in delicate crystal beauty and
amazing profusion on ceilings, walls, and floors. You'll marvel at
this stunning subterranean wonderland. Guided tours cover
about 1.5 miles underground. Wear comfortable shoes with rub-
ber soles. And bring your camera.

Facilities include camping, picnic grounds, fourth-eight RV hookups, showers, gift shop, and snack bar. "Biscuits" O'Bryan
charms young and old with cowboy poetry and frontier philoso-
phy as the host of the Covered Wagon Dinner Theater. The Wild
Bunch and a crusty collection of characters usually accompany
him at the Caverns of Sonora every Saturday evening from mid-
June through mid-August.

Location: About eight miles west on I-10; exit 392, Caverns of
Sonora Rd. (RM 1989), then about seven miles south

Hours: March 1 - September 30: daily 8:00 a.m. - 6:00 p.m.;
October 1 - February 28: 9:00 a.m. - 5:00 p.m.

SWEETWATER

Chamber of Commerce
915-235-5488
http://camalott.com/~sweetwater/index.html

SPECIAL EVENT

 ### RATTLESNAKE ROUNDUP

This town comes to life the second weekend in March for an out-of-the-ordinary celebration. The fun includes rattlesnake hunts, snake-handling and snake-milking demonstrations, a parade and "Miss Snake Charmer" contest, dance, 10-K run, and rattlesnake-eating contests.

Hill Country

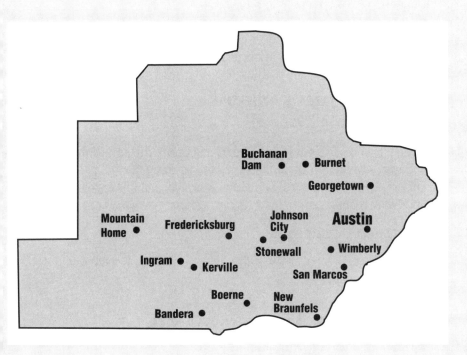

Buchanan Dam ●   ● Burnet

Georgetown ●

Mountain Home ●   Fredericksburg ●   Johnson City   Austin ●

Stonewall ●   Wimberly ●

Ingram ●   ● Kerville

San Marcos ●

Boerne ●

Bandera ●   New Braunfels ●

AUSTIN

Convention & Visitors Bureau
201 E. Second St.
800-926-2282 or 512-478-0098
http://www.austintexas.org

Due to the immense variety and number of kid-friendly attractions in major metropolitan areas, only a few are listed, and you're encouraged to visit the local Visitor Information Center for more detailed information.

> Ask for the brochure, "101 Things to Do in Austin."

AUSTIN CHILDREN'S MUSEUM

512-472-2499

Touch, play, and climb to your heart's content at this delightful children's museum. Its activities relate to three themes: "How Different People Live," "The Human Body," and "Everyday Science and Technology."

Location: 201 Colorado St.

Hours: Tuesday - Saturday 10:00 a.m. - 5:00 p.m., Sunday noon - 5:00 p.m.

AUSTIN NATURE AND SCIENCE CENTER

512-327-8180

Austin's only living science museum features a hands-on "Discovery Lab," the "Nature of Austin," showing Austin's four central ecosystems, and "Small Wonders," highlighting small reptiles, arthropods, and fish. Outdoor exhibits include animals that can't be returned to the wild and an "Eco-Detective Trail."

Location: 301 Nature Center Drive

Hours: Monday - Saturday 9:00 a.m. - 5:00 p.m., Sun, noon - 5:00 p.m.

Admission: FREE

AUSTIN ZOO

512-288-1490

www.austinzoo.com

Encounter many different animals at this delightful zoo in a Hill Country setting. Pony rides, train rides, and picnic area.

Location: US 290 west to Circle Dr., right on Circle Dr. to Rawhide Trail, right to entrance

Hours: Daily 10:00 a.m. - 6:00 p.m.

Admission: $5/adults, $4/children 2 to 12 and seniors, children under 2 free with paid adult; train ride and pony ride $2

CELEBRATION STATION

512-448-3533

Kids love this place. They can choose (or try them all) go-carts, batting cages with fast and slow pitching, bumper boats, a challenging miniature golf course, and games galore. There's even a food court.

Location: 4525 South I-35

Hours: Memorial Day - Labor Day opens daily at 10:00 a.m.; winter hours Monday - Thursday noon - 9:00 p.m., Friday noon - midnight, Saturday 10:00 a.m. - midnight, Sunday noon - 9:00 p.m.

Admission: All games priced individually

CONGRESS AVENUE BATS

512-327-9721
http://www.batcon.org

This is some bizarre tourist attraction! The nightly exodus of 1.5 million Mexican free-tail bats is among the most spectacular wildlife viewing opportunities in the country. The bats are in residence under Austin's Congress Avenue Bridge from mid-March to late October and typically emerge just before dusk. Bat Conservation International, headquartered in Austin, puts out *The Free-Tail Flyer,* a bat newsletter "by and for" the Congress Ave. bats and distributes lots of bat information and bat souvenirs. You can even "Adopt a Bat," if you wish.

> The 17 "Moonlight Towers" located throughout downtown Austin were erected in the 1890s to simulate a moonlight glow.

GOVERNOR'S MANSION

512-463-5518

It's exciting to see where the governor lives. This stately white-columned mansion has been the home of every Texas governor since it was built in 1856. The governor occupies a private apartment on the second floor. You won't get to see that, but the other elegant rooms and antique furnishings may be seen.

Location: 1010 Colorado St.

Hours: Public tours Monday - Friday every 20 minutes from 10:00 - 11:40 a.m.

HAMILTON POOL PRESERVE

512-264-2740

This grotto-like pool is one of Texas' most picturesque. A 60-foot waterfall spills into a deep, jade-green pool, a treasured

swimming hole for Austinites and University of Texas students. The water quality is carefully monitored, and swimming is not allowed when the bacteria count is too high, so call ahead. The area is also fun for picnicking and nature study.

Location: Texas 71 west approximately 16 miles to FM 3238, then south 13 miles

HILL COUNTRY FLYER

512-477-8468
http://www.main.org/flyer/index.html

Great fun for kids of all ages! This restored vintage steam excursion train runs through the beautiful Hill Country from Cedar Park to Burnet. Engine No. 786, a 75-year-old steam locomotive, pulls the train on a two-hour ride through scenic countryside. Following a short layover in Burnet, the train returns. Almost everyone on the train staff is a volunteer who devotes countless hours of time and shares a passion for preserving the era of the Iron Horse.

Location: The Cedar Park City Hall depot is near U.S. 183 and FM 1431

Hours: March - December: departures on Saturday and Sunday at 10:00 a.m.

Fares: Round-trip fares range from $10-$38

LADY BIRD JOHNSON WILDFLOWER CENTER

512-292-4200

Especially colorful in the springtime, this 42-acre site, founded by Lady Bird Johnson in 1982, is in the heart of the Hill Country. The grounds showcase research display gardens, landscaped areas, and theme gardens. The spacious facility includes a visitor

center with museum quality exhibits, a 240-seat auditorium, and five classroom-sized meeting areas.

Location: 4801 La Crosse Ave.

Hours: Tuesday - Sunday 9:00 a.m. - 6:00 p.m.

LAKE CRUISES

- Capital Cruises—Excursions on Town Lake and Lake Austin. Also pontoon, paddleboat, canoe, and kayak rental. 208 Barton Springs Rd. Seasonal—call for description of cruises and schedule: 512-480-9264

- Lone Star Riverboat—This working replica of an old-fashioned, double-decked, paddle wheel riverboat offers 1½-hour sight-seeing excursions on Town Lake from March through October. Call for description and schedule: 512-327-1388

- Flagship Texas—Lakeway—This 100-foot riverboat cruises beautiful Lake Travis at the Lakeway Resort and Conference Center. Open upper decks offer a spectacular view of the Texas Hill Country. 512-261-6484

PARKS

Austin's park system is phenomenal. Throughout the city, nine major park areas include more than 7,753 acres, including 5 municipal golf courses, 75 playgrounds, 44 swimming pools, 70 tennis court areas and 4 tennis centers, 15 community recreation centers, and 172 athletic fields. One of the most popular, Zilker Park, is listed below.

STATE CAPITOL COMPLEX

512-305-8400

Every Texan should see this massive, classic statehouse of famous Texas pink granite. It dominates the 46-acre, park-like setting of the complex. Completed in 1888, the Texas Capitol is the tallest in the United States. The magnificent building underwent major renovation in 1993-1994 and was restored to its original splendor. A new underground capitol extension was added during the renovation.

Daily tours include both facilities. The Capitol Complex Visitor Center is housed in the renovated General Land Office building constructed around 1857. It contains permanent and rotating exhibits, video presentation, a Texas gift shop, and the Texas Travel Information Center.

> In 1882 the state of Texas was far richer in land than cash. In exchange for building the state capitol building, the state granted 3,050,000 acres of land to a Chicago corporation.

Location: Congress and Eleventh St.

Hours: Tuesday - Friday 9:00 a.m. - 5:00 p.m., Saturday 10:00 a.m. - 5:00 p.m.; closed major holidays

ZILKER PARK

512-477-8672

Ride the miniature train, climb the Playscape, or cool off in Barton Springs pool. This lovely park in southwest Austin includes the popular Barton Springs swimming pool, eight miles of hiking/biking trails, Zilker Hillside Amphitheater, and Austin Area Garden Center. The theater presents shows under the stars from early June through August. The Garden Center is a free, beautiful showcase of flowers, shrubs and trees, a Japanese Garden and Rose Garden, and a pioneer log cabin furnished in frontier style.

CHUY'S MEXICAN RESTAURANT

512-836-3218

What a wonderfully outrageous place! There's lots of stuff to look at and special kids' food like macaroni and cheese. The Green Chili Festival in September sounds fantastic.

Location: 10520 N. Lamar

BANDERA

Convention & Visitors Bureau
1808 Texas 16 South
800-364-3833 or 830-796-3045

Claiming to be the "Cowboy Capital of the World," Bandera keeps the spirit of the Old West alive with rodeos, western-wear stores, and a downtown area that looks like a movie set from frontier times. Dozens of dude ranches and guest ranches are in the rolling hills around Bandera.

FRONTIER TIMES MUSEUM

830-796-3864

This museum houses a diverse collection of frontier relics including bottles from Judge Roy Bean's saloon. The collection of 500 bells from around the world adds an eccentric flair as does the museum's shrunken head from South America.

Location: 506 13th St.

Hours: Monday - Saturday 10:00 a.m. - 4:30 p.m., Sunday 1:00 - 4:30 p.m.

OLD SPANISH TRAIL (OST)

The OST is the local hangout. Dozens of John Wayne pictures make up the decor, along with saddles as barstools, and a covered wagon salad bar. They serve a dadgummed good chicken-fried steak, too.

DUDE RANCHES

Experience the real West! Staying on a dude ranch is exciting and fun for the whole family! Whether you call them dude ranches or guest ranches, Bandera has plenty. Some are rustic, others are equipped with all the modern conveniences. Check with the Convention & Visitors Bureau (above) for details. A few include:

DIXIE DUDE RANCH

800-375-Y'ALL (9255) or 830-796-4481
http://www.tourtexas.com/dixieduderanch/dixiedude.html

You'll be welcomed by the fifth generation on this working stock ranch founded by William Wallace Whitley in 1901. Situated on 725 acres, the Dixie Dude Ranch offers fine vistas of spectacular Texas Hill Country and modern comforts in the rooms, cabins, and spacious ranch headquarters. Explore the ranch on hiking trails, hunt for fossils and arrowheads, and enjoy a choice of planned activities such as horseback riding, swimming, hayrides, campfire sing-alongs, and lots of Western fun. When the chow bell rings, savor an outdoor barbecue, Sunday fried chicken, and an occasional cowboy breakfast served on the range.

THE FLYING L

800-292-5134
http://www.flyingl.com/

This is a 542-acre ranch situated on a beautiful 18-hole golf course. In operation since 1945, the Flying L's western charm has been retained as modern conveniences were added. The ranch offers a fun-filled activities program at the Kid's Korral for children three to twelve years old with story telling, pony rides, crafts, and Peewee Olympics. Horseback riding is for ages six and up, and corral rides for kids three to five. Other activities include nightly western-style entertainment, swimming pool, tennis courts, and water sports on the Medina River during the summer months. Meals are hearty and delicious and include a Texas-style barbecue and a fiesta Mexicana. Call for rates and special programs.

RUNNING-R GUEST RANCH

830-796-3984
http://www.rrranch.com/

The focus here is on horseback riding. The ranch's friendly cowboys will accompany you on rides through the ranch and the adjoining 5,500-acre Hill Country State Natural Area. They'll tell you something about the abundant wildlife and plants. Ride in a large arena where they offer riding lessons for beginners and advanced lessons for experienced riders. Play pool, ping-pong, volleyball, watch TV, swim, or sit on the porch and relax.

BOERNE

http://www.boerne.org/

CASCADE CAVERNS

830-755-8080

An impressive 90-foot underground waterfall was the inspiration for its name when it opened as a visitor attraction in 1932. Skilled guides provide one-hour interpretive tours on well-lighted, comfortable walking trails. The tour follows the main passage, which steadily enlarges until it ends in a spacious room highlighted by the namesake waterfall. A wet, active cave, it has huge rooms with lovely cave formations and crystal pools.

Location: I-10, exit 543, Cascade Caverns Road

Hours: Memorial Day - Labor Day: daily 9:00 a.m. - 6:00 p.m., winter Monday - Friday 10:00 a.m. - 4:00 p.m., Saturday and Sunday 9:00 a.m. - 5:00 p.m.

Admission: $6.95/adults, $4.95/children 3-11, $1/age 2 and younger; senior discount

CAVE WITHOUT A NAME

830-537-4212

Cave Without A Name is one of Texas' best-kept secrets, probably because of the lack of advertising and the slightly off-the-beaten-path location. It's one of the prettiest caves around.

Location: About six miles north on FM 474, turn right onto Kreutzberg Road, and follow the signs for about five miles to the cave.

Admission: $5/adults, $2/children 5-11

PO-PO FAMILY RESTAURANT

830-537-4194

Everyone loves this funky place with great food. An enormous collection of plates decorate the walls.

Location: Seven miles north of Boerne off I-10, exit 533

Hours: Daily 11:00 a.m. - 10:00 p.m.

GUADALUPE RIVER RANCH

800-460-2005 or 830-537-4837
http://www.guadalupe-river-ranch.com/

The kids will love all the activities—horseback riding and lessons, canoeing, river tubing, swimming, fishing, tennis, hayrides, game room, and animals. And the adults can stroll the grounds, laze by the Guadalupe River, nap in a swing, and just get away from it all. A variety of accommodations are available in different buildings on the 360-acre ranch. During the summer there's the GRR Adventure Club for kids ages four to twelve. An all-day program, it includes nature hikes, learning about plants and wildlife, arts and crafts projects, and a mid-day snack.

BUCHANAN DAM

INKS LAKE STATE PARK

http://www.tpwd.state.tx.us/park/parks.htm

Surrounding pretty little Inks Lake southeast of Buchanan Dam, this park offers camping, restrooms, picnic areas, fishing, swimming, boating, golf, nature study, and hiking.

Location: Texas 29 east, south on Park Rd. 4

BURNET

Chamber of Commerce
703 Buchanan Dr.
http://www.burnetchamber.org/

HILL COUNTRY FLYER—see: AUSTIN

LONGHORN CAVERNS STATE PARK

512-756-6976
http://www.tpwd.state.tx.us/park/parks.htm

Two miles of underground fantasy, this cave has a fascinating history. It has been the home of prehistoric cavemen, the site of secret gunpowder manufacture for Confederate armies, an outlaw hideout, dance hall, restaurant, and church. A little museum displays Indian artifacts, and frontier and Civil War items.

Location: About 11 miles southwest of Burnet via U.S. 281 and Park Rd. 4

Hours: Opens daily at 10:00 a.m.; tours last about 1½ hours

Admission: $6.50/adults, $4/children 5-12

VANISHING TEXAS RIVER CRUISE

800-474-8374 or 512-756-6986
http://vtrc.com/

This will undoubtedly be one of the highlights of your visit to the Texas Hill Country. On a sightseeing tour of the rugged Colorado River Canyon on Lake Buchanan, you'll see wildlife and beautiful scenery from the decks of the *Texas Eagle II*, a 70-foot, enclosed three-deck boat. April-June is wildflower season.

November-March is the time to see one of the largest colonies of American bald eagles that migrate to the Texas Colorado River canyon for the winter. Imagine seeing these majestic birds in flight or sitting on treetop perches.

Location: Three miles west on Texas 29, northwest 13½ miles on RM 2341

Hours: Call for cruise schedule and reservations

Admission: Prices range from $10-$15 for sightseeing cruises, higher for dinner and specialty cruises

FREDERICKSBURG

Convention & Visitors Bureau
106 N. Adams
830-997-6523
http://www.fredericksburg-texas.com/

German pioneers settled Prince Frederick's town and the surrounding countryside, and that heritage is abundantly evident today. Exceptionally wide streets allowed a team of oxen to make a U-turn. Unique to this area is the "Sunday House."

These tiny homes were used only on weekends when farm families came into town to conduct business on Saturday, then spend the night and go to church Sunday morning before returning to their farms. The native stone and timber "fachwerk" houses were built to last generations.

The scenic hills around Fredericksburg are brilliant with spectacular wildflowers each spring, and you'll find the best peaches anywhere in the summer months. The Germans enjoy life, and there's a celebration of some sort almost every weekend. You'll always find plenty of German food, music, and hospitality.

ADMIRAL NIMITZ MUSEUM AND HISTORICAL CENTER

830-997-4379

If one of your family members served in WW II, and you've heard the stories, this outstanding museum is a "must." Fleet Admiral Chester W. Nimitz was born in Fredericksburg in 1885. At his request, this historical center is dedicated to all who served with him during WW II. It consists of three sections: the restored Nimitz Steamboat Hotel, a famous frontier hotel (circa 1852) that houses the Museum of the Pacific War; the Garden of Peace, a gift from the people of Japan; and the History Walk, lined with aircraft, tanks, and guns.

Location: 304 E. Main St.

Hours: Daily 8:00 a.m. - 5:00 p.m.

DULCIMER FACTORY

See the oldest original American stringed instrument hand made from a variety of woods. The owner will show you around and tell you the history of the dulcimer.

Location: 715 S. Washington St.

Hours: Monday - Friday 10:00 a.m. - noon, 1:00 - 4:00 p.m.

ENCHANTED ROCK STATE PARK

915-247-3903

http://www.tpwd.state.tx.us/park/parks.htm

What a sight to see! This massive dome of solid granite was famous in Indian legends. It was said to be the site of human sacrifices. Some tribes feared to set foot on it; others used it as a rallying point because of its height. All held it in awe and reverence. The Indians believed ghost fires flickered on its crest on moonlit nights. A National Natural Landmark, the dome is 500 feet high and covers about 640 acres. A very popular site for hiking, rock climbing and rappelling, and picnicking; primitive camping in designated areas with reservations.

Location: Eighteen miles north off RM 965

FORT MARTIN SCOTT

This is the site of the first federal fort in Texas. It was established in 1848 (three years after Texas joined the U.S.) to guard the frontier from Indians, but German settlers had already arrived and established a treaty of friendship with the Comanche. Unique among treaties, it was never broken by either side. Because of this unusual trust, the fort became a center of trade among settlers, Indians, and soldiers.

The only original structure is the restored post guardhouse. A visitor center exhibits artifacts, documents, and a model of the fort, with plans for extensive restoration.

Location: Two miles east on U.S. 290

Hours: March - Labor Day: Wednesday - Sunday 9:00 a.m. - 5:00 p.m.; September - February: Friday - Sunday 9:00 a.m. - 5:00 p.m.

OLD TUNNEL WILDLIFE MANAGEMENT AREA

Bats! Over a million bats emerge from the tunnel each evening from June through October. You can watch this phenomenon and learn about bats on summer tours.

Location: About 10 miles south

PIONEER MUSEUM COMPLEX

830-997-2835

This outstanding complex features an eight-room furnished pioneer home and store built in 1849, a wine cellar and stein-hof (stone yard), a Victorian-style home, barn and blacksmith shop, smokehouse, an authentic Sunday House, log cabin, wagon shed, one-room schoolhouse, and a fire museum with early Fredericksburg fire-fighting equipment.

Location: 309 W. Main St.

Hours: Monday - Saturday 10:00 a.m. - 5:00 p.m., Sunday 1:00 - 5:00 p.m.

HILL TOP CAFE

830-997-8922

This former gas station/beer joint is just funky enough to be chic. The decor features an old jukebox and pinball machine and mounted deer heads on the wall. The food is outstanding, the menu an interesting combination of Texas-Cajun-Greek. You'll hear live jazz, blues, or boogie-woogie on the piano Friday and Saturday nights.

Hill Top Cafe
CHILDREN'S MENU

Location: Eleven miles northwest of Fredericksburg on U.S. 87

SCHMIDT BARN

830-997-5612

Schmidt Barn is one of the many guesthouses (gastehaus) in this tiny town. Representative of the area's early heritage, it allows a delightful return to the past. The small guesthouse, in a country setting, has thick stone walls and milled timber beams, a cozy sleeping loft bedroom (you'll have to flip to see who sleeps on the hide-a-bed downstairs), and collections of vintage toys, quilts, antique linens, and samplers.

SETTLERS CROSSING

800-874-1020
http://www.settlerscrossing.com

Meet Buster the donkey and see the flock of Russian Romanoff sheep roaming on thirty-five acres of rolling pastureland. Choose from seven private guesthouses on the property, each furnished with antiques and oversized beds; six have fireplaces, four have Jacuzzi tubs. Each guesthouse is rented separately and can accommodate from two to six.

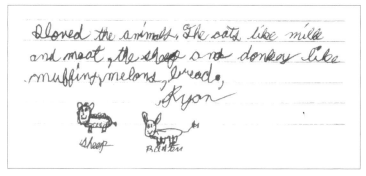

Excerpt from guest book of Settlers Crossing

GEORGETOWN

Convention & Visitors Bureau
800-436-8696 or 512-930-3545
http://www.georgetown.org/tourism/

INNER SPACE CAVERNS

512-863-5545
http://www.innerspacecavern.com/

Don't let the modern name and glitzy signs fool you—this is an exceptional cave. It's Texas' newest and most accessible cavern, a subterranean spectacle of stalactites, stalagmites, and flow-stones, where creative lighting dramatizes the natural beauty. You'll travel to the entrance via a unique subway and visit the world's first underground theatre. You'll also see the remains of prehistoric mastodons, wolves, and other Ice Age animals.

The cavern was discovered in the spring of 1963 by a Texas Highway Department core drilling team. Trying to learn if the ground was stable enough to support a highway overpass, they drilled a test hole, and the bit dropped twenty-six feet straight down.

Location: I-35, exit 259

Hours: Memorial Day - Labor Day: daily 9:00 a.m. - 6:00 p.m.; Labor Day - Memorial Day: 10:00 a.m. - 5:00 p.m.; closed two weeks prior to Christmas

Admission: $8/adults, $5/children 4-12, free for children under 4

THE CANDLE FACTORY

512-863-6025

Tour the candle factory and watch beautiful hand-dipped candles take shape while resident artists hand-finish wax figurines.

Location: I-35, exit 259

Hours: Monday - Saturday 9:00 a.m. - 5:30 p.m., Sunday 10:00 a.m. - 5:30 p.m.

GRUENE

http://www.gruene.net/index.htm

Now within the city limits of New Braunfels, the historic village of Gruene (pronounced "green") has been restored as a charming little town. Wander through all the artisan studios, boutique shops, antique shops, and fine restaurants. Gruene Hall, the oldest dance hall in Texas, circa 1880, regularly offers weekend performances by well-known country-western celebrities. Located on the Guadalupe River, Gruene is also an immensely popular recreational site for tubing and other water activities.

Location: Gruene Rd. off N. Loop 337

THE GRISTMILL

830-625-0684

Explore this three-story brick 1878 cotton gin with multi-level outdoor decks overlooking the Guadalupe River, tin-roofed patios nestled among the trees, and dining areas inside near a cozy fireplace. The innovative menu will appeal to adults, but the Gristmill has great burgers, too.

Location: Beneath the water tower in historic downtown Gruene

INGRAM

LAZY HILLS GUEST RANCH

800-880-0632 or 830-367-5600
http://www.lazyhills.com

Since 1959 the Steinruck family has been welcoming folks to Lazy Hills Guest Ranch, a 750-acre spread in the heart of the beautiful Texas Hill Country. They offer comfortable accommodations, delicious meals, and fun guest ranch activities— hayrides, cookouts, campfires, horseback riding, swimming, tennis, and nature trails.

Kids especially love the summer when supervised activities for children are provided. Free story telling, nature walks, songs, arts and crafts, and other activities keep hands and minds busy. A playground is always available.

JOHNSON CITY

see also: STONEWALL

EXOTIC RESORT ZOO

830-868-4357

Bring your camera and board one of the zoo's vehicles for close encounters with exotic animals from around the world. Located on 137 wooded acres, it also features a petting area where young animals love all the attention they get from young humans.

Location: Four miles north on U.S. 281

Hours: April - October: daily 9:00 a.m. - 6:00 p.m., November - March: daily 9:00 a.m. - 5:00 p.m.

LYNDON B. JOHNSON NATIONAL HISTORIC PARK

830-868-7128
http://www.nps.gov/lyjo/

The visitor center features information, exhibits, a bookstore, and audiovisual programs, as well as ranger talks and monthly guest lecturer programs. Down the street is the frame house where Lyndon Johnson lived while attending public school. Furnishings include Johnson family items and period furniture.

One block west via a nature trail is an old ranch complex called Johnson Settlement, owned by the president's grandfather and great-uncle from 1867-1872. The rustic 1856 dogtrot cabin, 1880 stone farm buildings, and pastures with grazing Texas longhorn cattle reflect its frontier heritage.

Location: Two blocks south of U.S. 290 between Avenues F and G

Hours: Daily except New Year's Day and Christmas

Admission: No fee to visit the Johnson City District, but donations are gratefully accepted; $3 fee to take the bus tour of the LBJ Ranch for persons who are seven years old or older; younger children are free

 ## PEDERNALES FALLS STATE PARK

830/868-7304
http://www.tpwd.state.tx.us/park/parks.htm

This park preserves the scenic natural beauty of the area, featuring picturesque waterfalls, abundant animal and bird life, fishing, swimming, camping, hiking, and nature study.

Location: About eight miles east via FM 2766

KERRVILLE

Convention & Visitors Bureau
800-221-7958
http://www.ktc.net/kerrcvb/

KERRVILLE CAMERA SAFARI

830-792-3600

Observe native and exotic animals from around the world as they roam over this drive-through Hill Country ranch. Don't forget your camera and binoculars.

Location: I-10 and Texas 16 (exit 508)

Hours: Open daily 9:00 a.m. - sunset

Admission: $6/adults, $5/seniors 62+, $4/children 3-11

LOUISE HAYS PARK

This small town park along the Guadalupe River offers old-fashioned fun for kids. Feed the ducks and geese, fly kites, swim, and fish.

Y.O. RANCH—see: MOUNTAIN HOME

MOUNTAIN HOME

Y.O. RANCH

800-YO-RANCH
830-640-3222
http://www.yoranch.com/

Head 'em up and move 'em out! The Y.O. Ranch has an annual
cattle drive. In the summer it has an outstanding Adventure
Camp, with different levels of activities and camping for youngsters and teenagers. Established in 1880, this vast ranch in the
scenic Hill Country is home to North America's largest collection of exotic wild animals—over fifty different species. A
substantial herd of Texas longhorns live here, too, and several
historic buildings are preserved.

You may visit for a day or spend an entire vacation. Daily tours (reservations required) include
lunch, and photo safaris are offered year round.
Various overnight accommodations are available, plus a swimming pool, nature trails,
horseback riding, and hayrides.

Location: Ranch entrance is fifteen miles west of Mountain
Home on Texas 41; ranch headquarters are eight miles north of
the entrance

NEW BRAUNFELS

Visitor Center
I-35 and Post Road
800-572-2626
www.nbcham.org

The city of New Braunfels offers unlimited water recreational activities along the Guadalupe and Comal Rivers. Dozens of outfitters rent tubes, canoes, and rafts. The numerous attractions, activities, rivers, excellent campgrounds, even several kid-friendly bed and breakfast establishments make this area great for family vacations.

You'll see evidence of the area's rich German heritage expressed everywhere—great German food, pride in workmanship, and celebrations of fun and festivity.

ALAMO CLASSIC CAR MUSEUM

830-606-4311

Take a trip down memory lane among one of the finest private collections of classic vehicles in the state. These restored vehicles depict more than eight decades of automotive history.

Location: I-35 south near city limits, exit 180 or 182

Hours: Daily 10:00 a.m. - 6:00 p.m.

Admission: $5/males, $4/females

CHILDREN'S MUSEUM

830-620-0939

Children of all ages enjoy hands-on exhibits, which include CMN-TV studio, a puppet palace, and other creative areas. Explore, touch, and discover. It's in Marketplatz, the discount

shopping mall, so this is a great place for dads and kids to play while moms shop.

Location: 183 I-35, exit 187

Hours: Monday - Saturday 9:00 a.m. - 5:00 p.m., Sunday 10:00 a.m. - 5:00 p.m.

Admission: $2.50, children under 1 free

GRUENE—see: GRUENE (city listing)

HUMMEL MUSEUM

800-456-4866 or 830-625-5636

The world's largest collection—more than 300 paintings and drawings of original art by Sister M. I. Hummel, the artist and inspiration for the famous figurines. Watch a 30-minute video showing how the figurines are created.

Location: 199 Main Plaza

Hours: Monday - Saturday 10:00 a.m. - 5:00 p.m., Sunday noon - 5:00 p.m.

Admission: $5/adults, $4.50/seniors, $3/children 6-18, children under 6 free

LANDA PARK

830-608-2160

> The Comal River is the shortest river in the world, starting and ending within the city limits of New Braunfels.

Kids love Landa Park where they can wade in the bubbling, crystal-clear springs at the place the Comal River originates. Catch polliwogs and crawfish or collect stones that have been worn smooth by the swiftly flowing water. Feed the ducks and geese; watch out for the nibbling squirrels, though. Ride the miniature train around the scenic

park. Fish or ride the paddleboats on the lake. Free admission to park, fee for rides.

NATURAL BRIDGE CAVERNS

210-651-6101
http://www.naturalbridgetexas.com/caverns/

Wind through a vast subterranean maze—gigantic rooms and corridors stretch more than a mile—leading to fantastic cave formations and an underground creek. Named for its 60-foot natural limestone bridge, this remarkable cave is 140 million years old and still growing. One of the seven Texas show caves, it has also been designated a U.S. Natural Landmark.

Natural Bridge Caverns—View from Inspiration Point
Photo courtesy of Natural Bridge Caverns

Location: 12 miles west via Texas 46 and FM 1863

Hours: Open daily at 9:00 a.m.; tours every thirty minutes; closed New Year's Day, Thanksgiving, and Christmas

Admission: $9/adults, $6/children 4-12

NATURAL BRIDGE WILDLIFE RANCH

830-438-7400
www.nbwildliferanchtx.com

Drive through this African safari, Texas style. Exotic, native, and endangered species roam freely in 200 acres of natural environment. You'll get a snack to feed the animals in case they wander up to your car (bet they will). Since the ranch has a highly

Natural Bridge Wildlife Park
Photo courtesy of New Braunfels Chamber of Commerce

successful breeding program, you'll probably get to see baby animals year round. There's also a snack bar and picnic area.

Location: I-35, exit 175; seven miles on Natural Bridge Caverns Rd.

Hours: Daily 9:00 a.m. - 5:00 p.m.; closed New Year's, Thanksgiving, and Christmas

Admission: $7.50/adults, $6.25/seniors, $5/children 3-11

SCHLITTERBAHN

830-625-2351
http://www.schlitterbahn.com/

Get ready for this one! Plan a full day at the state's largest waterpark with over 65 acres of family fun. Located along the

Schlitterban
Photo courtesy of New Braunfels Chamber of Commerce

banks of the Comal River, Schlitterbahn ("slippery road" in German) has something for everyone. With over forty rides and activities in six theme areas, there are tube chutes, river rapids, water slides, uphill water coasters, five swimming pools, hot tubs, five children's water playgrounds, volleyball courts, gift shops, restaurants, and cool, shady picnic grounds. Thrilling, award-winning high tech rides, such as the "Boogie Bahn" surfing wave and the "Dragon Blaster," offer hours of fun. Even toddlers can join in by building sandcastles on the beach or sliding down soft foam slides.

Location: 400 N. Liberty St.

Hours: Daily mid-May through mid-August; weekends spring and fall

Admission: All Day Pass: $25.28/adults and over 12, $20.84/children 3-11, free for children under 3

Half-Day Pass: $18.19/adults and over 12, $14.83/children 3-11, free for children under 3

SNAKE FARM

Kids, mostly boy kids, enjoy this place.

Location: I-35 just south of town

SPECIAL EVENTS

KINDERMASKENTAG (Children's Masquerade Day)—The first weekend in May is dedicated to children. The Children's Day Parade allows children to dress in wonderful costumes and parade through town. There are demonstrations of early pioneer activities such as quilting and soap making, dancing, and music.

WURSTFEST—In late October and/or early November, this is an annual, fun-filled ten-day salute to the sausage. For information or advance tickets, call 800-221-4369 or 830-625-9167 http://www.new-braunfels.com/wurstfest/

SAN MARCOS

Convention & Visitors Bureau
Visitor Center: I-35, exit 206
888-200-5620 or 512-353-3435
http://www.centuryinter.net/tourism/

San Marcos is renowned for the water recreation activities on the crystal clear San Marcos River. Scuba, snorkel, fish, kayak, or tube the river—the water is 72 degrees year round.

AQUARENA SPRINGS CENTER

800-999-9767

Although Ralph the Swimming Pig is gone and the amusement park rides are silent, the glass bottom boats still let you view the bubbling springs and the Natural Aquarium of Texas. Since the purchase of Aquarena Springs by Southwest Texas State University in 1994, this once-popular amusement park has become an educational facility. An Endangered Species exhibit gives visitors an up-close look at the unique species that live only in the San Marcos River. With the park's focus on nature, Aquarena Springs is a new spotlight for nature tourism.

Location: On Aquarena Springs Drive

Hours: Daily 9:30 a.m. - 6:00 p.m.

Admission: FREE; fee for glass-bottom boat rides: $5/adult, $4/seniors, $3/children 4-15

WONDER WORLD

512-392-3760
www.wonderworld-park.com

Another one-of-a-kind place! Fun and educational for the whole family, this is the only earthquake-formed cave in the U.S. that is open to the public. Unlike water-formed caves, it's not harmed by touch or light, and visitors may take photos and experience the cave close-up. In a dark room, minerals imbedded in the cave walls glow in various colors. The Tejas Observation Tower gives

Wonder World
Photo courtesy of Wonder World

an awesome view of the Balcones fault line and the city of San Marcos. You'll also enjoy a train ride, animal petting area, anti-gravity house, and gift shop.

Location: I-35, exit 202 to Wonder World Dr.

Hours: Summer: 8:00 a.m. - 8:00 p.m.; winter: 9:00 a.m. - 6:00 p.m.

Admission: Combination tickets: $13.95/adults, $9.95/children 4-11

STONEWALL

see also: JOHNSON CITY

LYNDON BAINES JOHNSON NATIONAL HISTORICAL PARK

830-868-7128
http://www.nps.gov/lyjo/

The LBJ Ranch rests along the banks of the Pedernales River in the heart of the Texas Hill Country. In the spring and summer wildflowers, so beloved by Lady Bird Johnson, bloom across the countryside with vibrant colors. The ranch tour begins at the LBJ State Park Visitor Center (see below) and includes the reconstructed Johnson birthplace, the family cemetery and final resting place of the president, the one-room Junction school-house, the "Texas White House," and a drive across the 600-acre ranch. It's operated by the National Park Service as part of the National Historic Park that includes Johnson's boy-hood home (see Johnson City).

Location: off U.S. 290, RR 1

Hours: Daily 10:00 a.m. - 4:00 p.m.; closed Christmas

Admission: Fee for tour of the ranch

LBJ STATE PARK

830/644-2252
http://www.tpwd.state.tx.us/park/parks.htm

A visitor center presents interpretive exhibits and serves as the starting point for the LBJ ranch tours (see above). There are also picnic facilities, a swimming pool, tennis courts, wildlife displays, and nature trails. The Sauer-Beckmann Farmstead is a living history museum where rural life as it was from 1900-1918 is interpreted. Kids enjoy seeing the guides in period costume perform daily chores and crafts of the early twentieth century.

Location: U.S. 290 just east of Stonewall

Hours: Daily 8:00 a.m. - 5:00 p.m.

WIMBERLEY

Visitors Center just north of Cypress Creek
Chamber of Commerce
512-847-2201

This is a quaint little town with lots of artists, specialty shops, and restaurants. Not many attractions especially for kids, but the Blanco River, nearby Canyon Lake, and Guadalupe River offer lots of water sports and tubing.

PIONEERTOWN

A village of the Old West is re-created at 7-A Ranch Resort on the Blanco River. Medicine shows and old-time melodramas are performed in the summer.

Location: 7-A Ranch Resort, one mile south of Wimberley

Hours: Summer: daily 10:00 a.m. - 10:00 p.m.; winter: Saturday - Sunday 1:00 - 5:30 p.m.

WIMBERLEY GLASS WORKS

512-847-9348

Local artists provide free glassblowing demonstrations complete with information on the history of glass.

Location: RR 12 south 1.6 miles from village square, left at 111 W. Spoke Hill Dr.

Hours: Thursday - Monday 10:00 a.m. - 5:00 p.m.

North Central

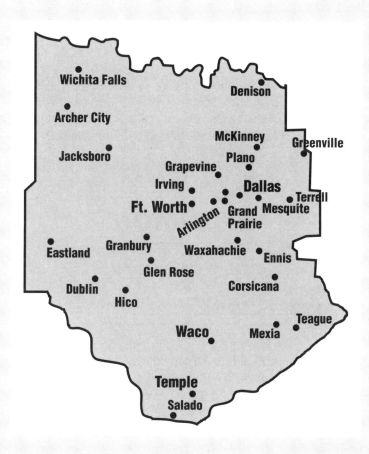

Wichita Falls

Denison

Archer City

McKinney

Greenville

Jacksboro

Plano

Grapevine

Irving

Dallas

Ft. Worth

Terrell

Arlington

Grand Prairie

Mesquite

Eastland

Granbury

Waxahachie

Ennis

Glen Rose

Corsicana

Dublin

Hico

Teague

Waco

Mexia

Temple

Salado

ARCHER CITY

BOOKED UP

940-574-2511

If you're a movie buff, you may want to drive down the main street of Archer City, the site of two movies based on novels written by Larry McMurtry: *The Last Picture Show* filmed in 1971 and *Texasville* filmed in 1989.

Native son Larry McMurtry, author of *Lonesome Dove*, has also collected books for several years. Now he's opened a bookstore, Booked Up, which claims the largest collection of antiquarian books in the U.S. It occupies renovated buildings on both sides of Main Street.

ARLINGTON

http://www.arlington.org/

AIR COMBAT CENTER

817-640-1886

Experience the thrill of being a military fighter pilot! Simulators are actual jet aircraft cockpits mounted on hydraulic motion bases that "pilots" control. Flights start with short ground school and mission briefing before suiting up in complete flight gear. Takes about 1½ hours.

Location: 921 Six Flags Dr. #117

Hours: Daily 9:00 a.m. - 5:00 p.m. Reservations advised. Minimum height, 4 feet 8 inches

THE BALLPARK IN ARLINGTON

Ticket office: 817- 273-5100
Tour information: 817-273-5099
Museum information: 817-273-5600
http://www.texasrangers.com/

What all-American kid doesn't like to hear the words, "take me out to the ballgame?" The Ballpark in Arlington is the home of the American League Texas Rangers, and what a ballpark it is. One of the finest facilities ever built for baseball, it's worthy of a visit whether or not the Rangers are playing.

This unique 270-acre complex includes the Legends of the Game Baseball Museum and Learning Center (see below), a four-story office building within the ballpark, a youth baseball park, a 12-acre lake, and parks and recreation space on the perimeter. You'll find Friday's Front Row Sports Grill, the Texas Rangers Souvenir Shop, luxury suites, and the private Diamond Club dining room. Total cost of the project was approximately $191 million.

> The Ballpark in Arlington seats 49,166 people.

Location: I-30 at Nolan Ryan Expressway or Ballpark Way exit

Hours: Home games from April - September with most starting at 7:30 p.m.

LEGENDS OF THE GAME BASEBALL MUSEUM AND LEARNING CENTER

817-273-5600

This museum exhibits baseball uniforms, equipment, baseball cards, photos, and statistics from Babe Ruth to Nolan Ryan, showing the history of this all-American sport. The Learning Center features interactive exhibits on baseball and how the sport relates to other fields. It's also possible to arrange school field trips, birthday parties, sleepovers, and youth programs.

101

Location: The Ballpark in Arlington

Hours: March - October: Monday - Saturday 9:00 a.m. - 7:30 p.m. Call for November - February hours

RIVER LEGACY PARKS AND LIVING SCIENCE CENTER
817-860-6752
http://www.ci.arlington.tx.us/nature.html

Hiking/biking trails, nature trails, river overlooks, and picnic areas are found within these parks along the riverbanks of the Trinity River.

The Living Science Center features interactive exhibits and displays including terrariums, aquariums, and a map of Texas rivers. A simulated raft ride uses the latest technology to make it an exciting ride down the Trinity River.

Location: 703 NW Green Oaks Blvd.

Hours: Science Center Tuesday - Saturday 9:00 a.m. - 5:00 p.m.

Admission: FREE for parks; fee for Science Center

SIX FLAGS OVER TEXAS
817-640-8900
http://www.sixflags.com/parks/

This famed 200-acre theme park features fun and fantasy in lavish landscaped settings. Breathtaking rides include the "Texas Giant," a massive wooden roller coaster voted three times the top roller coaster in the world, and the "Texas Chute-Out," a 17-story parachute drop. New in 1998 is "Mr. Freeze" that launches riders to speeds of 70 mph in less than four seconds and to a height of 236 feet—not for the faint of heart.

For the nostalgic visitor the "Silver Star," an elegant mid-1920s carousel restored to all its grandeur, is just behind the park's landmark flags and fountain. Special shows, musical revues, a popular stunt show, and puppet theater performances are included with all the rides on an all-inclusive admission ticket.

The Six Flags of Texas
Spain 1519-1685; 1690-1821
France 1685-1690
Mexico 1821-1836
Republic of Texas 1836-1845
Confederacy 1861-1865
United States 1845-1861; 1865-present

Special events include "Fright Fest" at Halloween with ghosts and goblins and haunted houses, and "Holiday in the Park" at Christmastime, a glittering wonderland featuring musicals, ice shows, and a giant sledding hill.

Location: I-30 and Texas 360

Hours: Daily in summer, weekends spring and fall

SIX FLAGS HURRICANE HARBOR

817-265-3356
http://www.sixflags.com/parks/

Wear the kids out with acres of sun and fun! Built for little kids as well as big kids, there are rides and slides and flumes for everyone with 22 rides on 47 acres.

Location: 1800 Lamar Blvd., adjacent to Six Flags Over Texas amusement park

Hours: Mid-May through mid-September

OTHER:

Arlington Skatium - the largest freestanding skating center in the country - 5515 South Cooper Street - 817-784-6222

AMF Arlington Lanes - 24 championship lanes, bumper bowling for the kids, Laser Tron, and

the latest in video games - 1801 East Lamar Blvd. - 817-276-9898

Big Wheels Skateland - skate, in-line skate, play roller hockey, lessons - 1118 California Lane - 817-467-7744

Chuck E. Cheese - a pizza place with the "Chuck E. Shuffle" show, games, and rides -2216 South Fielder Rd. - 817-861-1562 and 3200 Justiss Dr. - 817-649-2933

Dyno-Rock Indoor Climbing Gym - climbing for all ages and skill levels in a safe, controlled environment - 608 East Front St. - 817-461-3966

Mountasia Fantasy Golf - 54-hole miniature golf course with caves, waterfalls, and other challenging obstacles, and a 7,000-square-foot clubhouse with the latest video games - off I-30 - 817-460-3600

CORSICANA

COLLIN STREET BAKERY

800-248-3366

Possibly the world's most famous fruitcake has been baked by Collin Street Bakery since 1896 and marketed under the name "Deluxe." It's shipped each year to every state in the nation and more than 190 foreign lands and is the only fruit-cake granted the rare Gourmet Society Culinary Merit Award.

Location: 401 W. Seventh St.

Hours: Monday - Friday 8:00 a.m. - 6:00 p.m.

PIONEER VILLAGE

This village of restored houses and buildings from mid-1800s features homes, stores, a doctor's office, blacksmith shop, covered wagon, and stagecoach.

Location: 912 W. Park Ave.

Hours: Monday - Saturday 9:00 a.m. - 5:00 p.m., Sunday 1:00 - 5:00 p.m.

DALLAS

Convention & Visitors Bureau
1201 Elm Street
800-C-DALLAS or 214-571-1000
http://www.dallascvb.com/

Due to the immense variety and number of kid-friendly attractions in this vast metropolitan area, only a few are listed, and you are encouraged to get a copy of the book *Exploring Dallas with Children* and visit the local Visitor Information Center for more detailed information.

DALLAS COWBOYS—see: IRVING

DALLAS FIREFIGHTERS MUSEUM

The old 1884 horse-drawn steamer, the last one used in the city, is on exhibit here. So is a 1936 Texas Centennial ladder truck and other fire memorabilia. More than one hundred years of Dallas history is housed in this old two-story fire station, circa 1907.

Location: 3801 Parry Ave., across from Fair Park

Hours: Monday - Friday 9:00 a.m. - 4:00 p.m.

DALLAS ZOO

214-670-5656
http://dallas-zoo.org/

Look for the 67½-foot bronze and Plexiglas giraffe near the entrance. The legs are 25 feet long, the body is 22 feet long and 10' 2" wide, and the head and neck are a total of 32 feet.

The Dallas Zoo is home to more than 2,000 animals, including many rare and endangered species, a nationally renowned

> The Plexiglas giraffe near the zoo's entrance is the tallest statue in the state.

reptile collection, interactive Reptile Discovery Center, and walk-through rain forest aviary. Within the zoo is a 25-acre "Wilds of Africa" exhibit, featuring numerous species of African birds, mammals, and reptiles roaming in naturalistic recreations of native habitat, picnic areas, a gift shop, and year-round special events.

Location: I-35E, at the Marsalis exit, about three miles south of downtown

Hours: Daily 9:00 a.m. - 5:00 p.m.; closed Christmas Day

Admission: $6/adult 12-64, $4/seniors, $3/children 3-11; free for children under 3

FAIR PARK

Built for the 1936 Texas Centennial, Fair Park, located east of downtown Dallas was recognized in 1986 as a National Historic Landmark for its outstanding Art Deco architecture. It's the home of the Texas State Fair each fall; the rest of the year it serves as a popular city park, including the following attractions:

- AGE OF STEAM MUSEUM
  214-428-0101
  http://www.startext.net/homes/railroad/musmain.htm

Enjoy a wonderful, nostalgic look at the heyday of railroading.

Hours: Thursday - Friday 10:00 a.m. - 3:00 p.m., Saturday - Sunday 11:00 a.m. - 5:00 p.m.

- COTTON BOWL STADIUM
The stadium seats 70,030 for college football games and the Cotton Bowl game on New Year's Day.

- DALLAS AQUARIUM AT FAIR PARK
214-670-8443

See the amazing "Amazon Flooded Forest" exhibit, watch the piranha feeding, and visit a varied collection of more than 375 species of aquatic animals.

Hours: Daily 9:00 a.m. - 4:30 p.m.; closed Thanksgiving and Christmas

- DALLAS MUSEUM OF NATURAL HISTORY
214-421-3466
http://www.dallasdino.org/

This fine museum includes the largest exhibition of Texas wildlife habitats and the world's first reconstructed Texas dinosaur. The huge research museum features excellent permanent exhibits as well as special exhibits and events throughout the year. It offers classes, workshops, field trips, and family programs.

Hours: Daily 10:00 a.m. - 5:00 p.m.; closed Thanksgiving Day and Christmas Day

Admission: $5/adults, $3/children 3-18 and seniors, free for children under 3; FREE admission every Monday from 10:00 a.m. - 1:00 p.m.

- THE SCIENCE PLACE AND IMAX THEATER
214-428-5555
http://www.scienceplace.org/

The Science Place makes learning interesting and fun. It's where kids of all ages can learn why and how things work—

where kids can use their senses of touch, sight, hearing, smell, and their imagination to understand the wonders of science and mathematics. Children and their parents or grandparents can experience the thrill of discovery through hands-on exhibits, workshops, and special programs. Kid's Place is a special place for little ones, and there's also a planetarium, store, and cafe.

The IMAX Theater uses state-of-the-art equipment to show films on a 79-foot overhead dome.

Hours: Daily 9:30 a.m. - 5:30 p.m.; closed Christmas

SAMUELL FARM—see: MESQUITE

The first automatic traffic signals in the United States were installed in Dallas in 1923.

SIXTH FLOOR

http://www.jfk.org/

This exhibition on the life, death, and legacy of President John F. Kennedy displays photographs, artifacts, a 30-minute audio tour, and six films. The Visitor Center at the former Texas School Book Depository has elevators up to the Sixth floor.

Location: 411 Elm St.

Hours: Daily 9:00 a.m. - 6:00 p.m.; closed Christmas

Admission: Regular tour: $5/adults, audio tour: $7/adults, children under 12 half price

SOUTHFORK RANCH—see: PLANO

WEST END MARKETPLACE

This cheerful market has dozens of shops, restaurants, and night clubs including Planet Hollywood. Activity is always going on, whether special events or street entertainers.

Location: In the Historic District at the north end of Market St. in downtown Dallas.

MEDIEVAL TIMES

214-761-1800

Cheer for your favorite knight as you dine. Visit the Middle Ages and enjoy all the pageantry of a medieval feast, including horsemanship, falconry, sorcery, and an authentic jousting tournament. Call for information, reservations, and show times.

Location: 2021 N. Stemmons Fwy. (I-35E)

SPORTS

Dallas Cowboys - football - 556-9900

Dallas Mavericks - basketball - 748-1808

Dallas Sidekicks - indoor soccer - 653-0200

Texas Rangers - baseball - 817-273-5100

Dallas Burn - outdoor soccer - 373-8000

Dallas Freeze - hockey - 631-7825

Dallas Dragoons - polo - 979-0300

Dallas Stars - ice hockey - 868-2890

DENISON

http://www.denisontx.com/

HAGERMAN NATIONAL WILDLIFE REFUGE

Lake Texoma offers food and a rest haven for migrating and wintering waterfowl. Over three hundred species of birds have been recorded on this 11,300-acre refuge. Huge flocks of birds pass through each spring and fall. The Visitor Center has interpretive displays and information.

Location: From U.S. 75 between Denison-Sherman, take FM 691 west to county airport, FM 1417 north 1½ miles, follow the sign west to refuge

RED RIVER RAILROAD MUSEUM AND KATY DEPOT

903-463-6238

 The grand Katy Depot was the home of the MKT (Missouri-Kansas-Texas) Railroad for over 85 years. This museum is the official repository of historical records and artifacts of the Katy Railroad Historical Society. Exhibits feature photographs, artifacts, and railroad equipment. A diesel engine, caboose, a vintage gondola car, and tank cars are on exhibit outside. The old Katy Depot now houses restaurants, specialty shops, and professional offices.

Location: 101 E. Main St. in the old Katy Depot

Hours: Monday - Saturday 10:00 a.m. - 1:00 p.m. and 2:00 - 4:00 p.m.

DUBLIN

DR PEPPER BOTTLING COMPANY

254-445-3466
http://drpep.com/

Tour the "Oldest Dr Pepper Bottling Company." Opened in 1891, the bottling plant in Dublin was the very first franchise. It's now the only place in the world that still uses the original formula with pure cane sugar instead of artificial sweeteners. Bottling is done on Tuesday. There's a restored soda fountain and a little museum with Dr Pepper memorabilia.

Location: 221 S. Patrick

Hours: Monday - Friday 8:00 a.m. - 5:00 p.m.

EASTLAND

http://www.eastland.net/eastland/

"OLD RIP"

A Texas horned frog was sealed in the cornerstone of the Eastland courthouse built in 1897, according to apparently authentic records. In 1928 when the new courthouse was built, the cornerstone was opened, and the horned frog was still alive! Named "Old Rip," he received great publicity and was displayed nationally. When he died, he was placed on purple velvet and white satin in a glass-front casket and lies in state in the present Eastland County Courthouse.

POST OFFICE MURAL

An incredible 6' x 10' mural of postage stamps, which resembles a stained-glass window, shows post office history. Former postmaster, the late Marene Johnson-Johnson spent seven years and used over 11,000 stamps to painstakingly assemble the mosaics of historical scenes and famous stamps.

Location: 411 Main at the post office

ENNIS

http://www.visitennis.org/

RAILROAD AND CULTURAL HERITAGE MUSEUM

972-875-1901

Once Ennis was the hub for the Houston and Texas Central Railroad. Memorabilia include an 1897 edition of the "Book of Rules for Train Operators" and miniature replicas of the train station in its heyday.

Location: 105 Main St.

TEXAS MOTORPLEX

214-875-2641

This racetrack presents amateur and professional drag racing throughout the year. It attracts some of the top names in racing, and the Chief National is held every October. The facility seats 39,000.

Location: U.S. 287, between I-45 and I-35E

FORT WORTH

Fort Worth Convention & Visitors Bureau
415 Throckmorton in Sundance Square
800-433-5747, 817-336-8791
and
130 E. Exchange Ave. in Historic Stockyards District
http://www.fortworth.com/

Fort Worth, "where the West begins," keeps the spirit of the Old West alive in the historic Stockyards district. It's also acclaimed for it's cultural district and the magnificently restored downtown area, Sundance Square.

CASA MANANA PLAYHOUSE

817-332-2272
http://www.iminet.com/casamanana/

Casa Manana has great children's shows during the summer. The huge geodesic dome marks the spot of one of the nation's most notable theaters-in-the-round, featuring dramas and musical comedies throughout the year. Call for schedule, tickets, and shows.

Location: 3101 Lancaster

FIRE STATION NO. 1

817-732-1631

The exhibit "150 Years of Fort Worth" showcases the city's colorful history. It's located in the first fire station building.

Location: Commerce and Second Streets downtown

Hours: Daily 9:00 a.m. - 7:00 p.m.

FORT WORTH MUSEUM OF SCIENCE AND HISTORY AND OMNI THEATER

817-732-1631
http://www.fwmuseum.org/

This world-class museum has excellent permanent displays and traveling exhibits. Over 100,000 artifacts and specimens are available for research and exhibition.

KIDSPACE is an indoor discovery area designed for youngsters age two to six. "DinoDig" encourages them to become amateur paleontologists and dig for dinosaur bones in a large outdoor discovery area.

Omni Theater's curved screen surrounds you as you dive beneath the ocean, soar through the clouds, or possibly witness the launch of a space shuttle. Several different films are shown each week.

Astronomy programs are presented regularly in the Noble Planetarium.

Call for information and schedules for the Omni Theater and Noble Planetarium. All facilities are wheelchair accessible.

Location: 1501 Montgomery St.

Hours: Monday 9:00 a.m. - 5:00 p.m., Tuesday - Thursday 9:00 a.m. - 8:00 p.m., Friday and Saturday 9:00 a.m. - 9:00 p.m., Sunday noon - 8:00 p.m.

Admission: Museum: $6/adults, $4/seniors and children

FORT WORTH NATURE CENTER AND REFUGE

817-237-1111

This 3,500-acre refuge offers an interpretive center, as well as hiking and self-guided nature trails. You'll often see white-tailed deer or part of the bison herd.

Location: Ten miles northwest on Texas 199

Hours: Tuesday - Friday 9:00 a.m. - 5:00 p.m., Saturday 7:00 a.m. - 5:00 p.m., Sunday noon - 5:00 p.m.

FORT WORTH ZOO

817-871-7050
http://www.rwnet.com/FWZoo/

This exceptional zoo was selected as one of the top five zoos in America. You can easily spend a whole day here. See featured exhibits, including an African savanna at the edge of a forest with groups of endangered black and white rhinos, giraffes, and African birds in a natural setting.

Fort Worth Zoo
Photo courtesy of Fort Worth Convention & Visitors Bureau

The Herpetarium is acclaimed for its naturalistic exhibits and collection of frogs, turtles, crocodiles, and hundreds of snakes.

Asian Falls is carved out of an existing hillside and allows visitors to stroll on a raised boardwalk through a natural setting of grassy hills, waterfalls, and trees. You'll see Sumatran tigers and bears.

The World of Primates has all the great ape species and includes an indoor tropical rain forest with gorillas, monkeys, and free-flying tropical birds. Connecting outdoor exhibits feature other primates including chimpanzees, orangutans, gibbons, and bonobos.

Raptor Canyon features seven species of raptors including Andean condors, king vultures, bateleur eagles, and bald eagles. The Asian Rhino Ridge includes Asian greater one-horned rhinos, cranes, and deer.

The longest miniature train ride in the state begins opposite the zoo and winds through Forest and Trinity Parks. There's also a great gift shop and snack bar.

Location: University Dr. in Forest Park

Hours: Daily 10:00 a.m. - 5:00 p.m.; extended hours seasonally

Admission: $7/adults, $3.50/children ages 3-12, free for children 2 and under

LOG CABIN VILLAGE

817-926-5881

You can explore a "village" of seven authentic pioneer homes from the 1850s and see frontier tools, implements, and furnishings.

Location: University Dr. and Colonial Parkway in Forest Park

Hours: Tuesday - Friday 9:00 a.m. - 4:30 p.m., Saturday 10:00 a.m. - 4:30 p.m., Sunday 1:00 - 4:30 p.m.

Pate Museum of Transportation

http://www.classicar.com/museums/pate/pate.htm

There's lot to explore at this large indoor/outdoor museum—vintage and classic automobiles, military aircraft, a Navy minesweeper, an antique luxury railroad car, and many other exhibits. If you're interested, you can use the 1,500-volume research library of transportation books.
An annual old car swap meet brings over 200,000 participants from around the country.

Location: U.S. 377, 20 miles southwest in Cresson

Hours: Tuesday - Sunday 9:00 a.m. - 5:00 p.m.

Admission: FREE

Six Flags Over Texas—see: Arlington

Stockyards National Historic District

http://www.ftworthstockyards.com/

This is unequivocally the best place to experience the legends of the Old West. Along Exchange Avenue you can watch hats and boots being crafted, shop for western souvenirs, and eat authentic Tex-Mex food or a Texas-sized steak. You can attend an exciting rodeo, watch a cattle auction, or learn the Texas two-step. Visit Billy Bob's Texas (http://www.billybobstexas.com/), the world's biggest honky-tonk, open during the day for tourists. The Stockyards are located in Fort Worth's north side area of downtown at North Main and Exchange Avenue.

Fort Worth Historic Stockyards
Photo courtesy of Fort Worth Convention & Visitors Bureau

Fort Worth Stockyards Station
Photo courtesy of Fort Worth Convention & Visitors Bureau

STOCKYARDS STATION

http://www.flash.net/~stockyds/

Shop where sheep used to stay at Stockyards Station, a 165,000-square-foot shopping area in the renovated hog and sheep pens. Now filled with restaurants, shops, and galleries featuring a variety of western-oriented shops, it also includes the Tarantula steam train station (see below).

Location: 140 E. Exchange Ave.

STOCKYARDS CHAMPIONSHIP RODEO

817-625-1025
http://www.cowtowncoliseum.com/

Professional cowboys and cowgirls compete most weekends throughout the year in the air-conditioned comfort of Cowtown

Fort Worth Stockyards Rodeo
Photo courtesy of Fort Worth Convention & Visitors Bureau

Coliseum in the Stockyards, where Pawnee Bill's Wild West Show is also featured.

> Fort Worth boasts the state's largest purse for professional rodeo competition.

Location: 123 E. Exchange Ave.

Hours: Fridays and Saturdays at 8:00 p.m.

Admission: $8/adults, $6/children under 12

TARANTULA RAILROAD—see also: GRAPEVINE

817-625-RAIL or 800-952-5717
http://www.tarantulatrain.com/

This meticulously restored steam excursion train makes daily round-trips between Grapevine and Fort Worth's Stockyards Station. The Grapevine turn-around is on a 1927 Santa Fe Railroad turntable. Train schedule varies seasonally.

Location: Ticket office 140 E. Exchange Ave.

Fares: $19.95/adults, $9.95 children 3-12

SUNDANCE SQUARE

http://www.sundancesquare.com/

This area in downtown Fort Worth is an interesting contrast of renovated Victorian buildings nestled among glass and steel skyscrapers. The entertainment district contains a variety of art galleries, boutiques, restaurants, theaters, and upscale night spots. Kids will particularly enjoy the new multi-unit movie theater. Billy Miner's Saloon serves great hamburgers.

TEXAS MOTOR SPEEDWAY

817-215-8500
http://ask.simplenet.com/racing/tms.htm

Quite a sight to behold! The second-largest sports facility in the country offers dual banked turns, which allows the speedway to host both Indy-style racing and NASCAR Winston Cup stock cars. It's so vast that eight Texas Stadiums (home of the Dallas Cowboys) would fit in the infield of the raceway. Races and special events are scheduled throughout the year.

Location: I-35W and Texas 114

Water Gardens
817-871-8700

This unusual park features a conglomeration of pools, sculptures, and fountains, where you can stand 38 feet below the street and experience 1,000 gallons of water cascading down a 710-foot wall. Scenes from the sci-fi movie *Logan's Run* were filmed here. Splash and play in it or just watch everyone else.

Location: South end of downtown

Admission: FREE

Special Event

Fort Worth Stock Show and Rodeo - January
http://www.fwstockshowrodeo.com/

Festive fun awaits everyone at the nation's oldest continually held livestock show and the world's first and best indoor rodeo. Enjoy innumerable special attractions like the free nightly western roundup show, a five-acre carnival midway, western-theme exhibits, and all the food you can imagine.

The Western Classic Rodeo is a great favorite of rodeo fans, celebrating Fort Worth's rich heritage with pageantry, music, and western showmanship, sure to enthrall the entire family.

GLEN ROSE

Convention & Visitors Bureau
888-346-6282 or 254-3081

DINOSAUR VALLEY STATE PARK

254-897-4588
http://www.tpwd.state.tx.us/park/parks.htm

> The acrocanthosaurus and pleurocoelus tracks here are estimated to be 111-million years old.

The first sauropod tracks in the world were discovered here. Sauropods were 60-foot-long plant-eating reptiles that weighed up to thirty tons. Near Glen Rose, the Paluxy River flows over solid rock that contains the best-preserved dinosaur tracks in Texas. Now a unique, picturesque state park occupies this scenic area of the Paluxy River with interpretive exhibits that offer a glimpse of how Texas might have looked 100 million years ago. The 1,204-acre park also offers camping, picnicking, and nature trails.

Location: U.S. Highway 67 to FM 205, four miles to Park Road 59, then one mile to the headquarters

Hours: Daily 8:00 a.m. - 5:00 p.m.

FOSSIL RIM WILDLIFE CENTER

254-897-2960
http://www.fossilrim.com/

Bring your camera! You'll see animals you've never heard of before. At one of the country's most renowned facilities, some of the world's most endangered animal species roam free through

3,000 acres of unspoiled countryside. Fossil Rim has a world-famous breeding program for the cheetah and white rhino, the nation's second largest red wolf population, and over 1,000 exotic and endangered animals.

Other attractions include a petting pasture, cafe overlooking the valley, picnic area, nature trail, education center, and outstanding nature store. If you've got the time, inquire about the Foothills Safari Camp—a three-day, two-night behind-the-scenes adventure available only by advance reservations.

Location: Off U.S. 67, 3.5 miles west

Hours: Daily 9:00 a.m. - two hours before sunset; closed Thanksgiving and Christmas

GRANBURY

Convention and Visitors Bureau
100 North Crockett
800-950-2212 or 817-573-5548
http://www.granbury.org

Granbury's historic town square was the first in Texas to be listed in the National Register of Historic Places. Today the square is lined with gift and boutique shops, restaurants, antique shops, the Great Race Museum, and the Opera House. You can have an old-fashioned soda at Rinky Tink's or Granbury Sampler. This town knows how to have fun, and you'll probably find some kind of festival or celebration going on when you visit. The Great Race in April, Harvest Moon Festival in October, Civil War reenactments, and a candlelight Christmas tour are but a few.

> The smallest state park in the U.S. is the gravesite of Elizabeth Crockett, second wife of Davy Crockett. It's about six miles east of Granbury on U.S. 377 and FM 167.

BRAZOS DRIVE-IN THEATER

817-573-1311

Pile the family in the car, pack your snacks, and go to this authentic 1950s drive-in movie—one of only twelve still in operating in Texas.

Location: 1800 W. Pearl

Hours: Friday - Sunday: Opens at 9:00 p.m. during daylight savings time; otherwise open at 7:45 p.m.

GRANBURY OPERA HOUSE

817-573-9191

Traveling vaudeville acts, minstrel shows, and melodramas are gone, but the Granbury Opera House, originally built in 1889, was meticulously restored and reopened in 1975. Today the Opera House presents plays, musicals, and comedy revues on weekends.

Location: On the historic town square

Hours: February - December; call for information

GREAT RACE HALL OF FAME

817-573-5200
http://www.greatrace.com/

If you're a car buff, don't miss this. Exhibits change annually and may include cars with the Victorian lines of the 1910s or the graceful Art Deco curves of the 1920s and 1930s. Experience the thrills as you watch the video about the Great Race.

Location: 14 N. Crockett on the town square

Hours: Monday - Friday 10:00 a.m. - 5:00 p.m., Saturday 10:00 a.m. - 6:00 p.m., Sunday noon - 5:00 p.m.

THE GULCH AT GRANBURY

817-579-1515

This family entertainment park features a Texas-size miniature golf course, golf driving range, baseball/softball batting cages, arcades, and sand volleyball courts. The landscaped park has picnic pavilions and a snack bar.

Location: 5100 U.S. 377

Hours: Varies seasonally

THE JAIL AND HOOD COUNTY HISTORICAL MUSEUM

817-573-5548

The original cell blocks and hanging tower are still here. In fact, this old jail built in 1885 operated as a jail through 1978. Eye-opening stories and displays of artifacts and memorabilia depict the history of Granbury and Hood County. You'll find out how jails got the nickname "the slammer" when you enter one of the cells and the big iron doors slam shut behind you.

Location: 208 N. Crockett

Hours: Friday - Sunday afternoons

 ### LAKE GRANBURY

This scenic lake offers boating, fishing, water skiing, canoeing, and swimming. Four parks provide boat ramps, swimming, camping, and picnic areas. Several companies rent canoes, boats, jet-skis, and other water recreational equipment. Cruises on the lake are fun during the summer.

RAILROAD DEPOT MUSEUM

Restored to its 1914 style, the depot is representative of early twentieth century rural Texas train stations. Primarily used to house Hood County genealogical records, there is one room with railroad memorabilia. Saturdays, it's staffed by volunteers who give tours, tell stories, and answer questions about the Iron Horse era.

Location: 109 E. Ewell

Hours: Saturday 10:00 a.m. - 3:00 p.m.

GRAND PRAIRIE

PALACE OF WAX AND RIPLEY'S BELIEVE IT OR NOT!

214-263-2391
http://www.tourtexas.com/ripleys/palaceofwax.html

Meet remarkably life-like wax figures face to face—from movie stars to western legends to historical heroes. The exhibits place characters in realistic settings, such as in Dr. Blood's Asylum of Fear. You may see the resident sculptor at work in his studio.

The unusual, bizarre, and unbelievable displays in Ripley's Believe It or Not! are from the collection of a man who assembled some of the world's most curious oddities from around the world. Discover the art and weapons of a primitive people in the ruins of a secret temple or experience an earthquake. You may find yourself on the ocean floor in the undersea world of Atlantis. Hold onto your hat as you step into a Texas tornado and emerge safely to see what 200-mph winds can do.

Location: 601 E. Safari Parkway, exit Belt Line Rd. from I-30 between Dallas and Fort Worth

Hours: Memorial Day - Labor Day: 10:00 a.m. - 9:00 p.m.; remainder of year: Monday - Friday 10:00 am - 5:00 p.m., Saturday and Sunday 10:00 a.m. - 6:00 p.m.

GRAPEVINE

Convention and Visitors Bureau
One Liberty Park Plaza
Visitor Center
701 S. Main St. in the historic Cotton Belt Depot
800-457-6338 or 817-410-3185
http://www.ci.grapevine.tx.us/

GRAPEVINE OPRY

817-481-8733

The renovated historic Palace Theater is now a showcase of country and western entertainment. There's a foot-stompin', hand-clappin' family-style show every Friday and Saturday night that features local, regional, and national artists.

Location: 308 S. Main St.

GRAPEVINE MILLS MALL

972-724-4900
http://www.grapevinemills.com/

If the kids enjoy shopping, this is the place. The 1½ million-square-foot mall is one of the largest shopping centers in Texas and offers a variety of retail stores, outlets, restaurants, and entertainment arcades.

TARANTULA RAILROAD—see also: FORT WORTH

817-625-RAIL or 800-952-5717
http://www.tarantulatrain.com/

This meticulously restored steam
excursion train makes daily round-
trips between Grapevine and Fort
Worth's Stockyards Station. The
Grapevine turn-around is on a 1927 Santa Fe Railroad turntable.
The Grapevine Cottonbelt Depot is located at 707 S. Main.

GREENVILLE

Chamber of Commerce
2713 Stonewall Street
903-455-1510
http://www.greenville-chamber.org/

AMERICAN COTTON MUSEUM

903-450-4502

Cotton played a big part in Texas history. This museum displays
artifacts and memorabilia pertaining to the area's cotton industry. Learn about the planting, growing, ginning, bailing, spinning,
and weaving of cotton. Other exhibits include tributes to the
county's celebrities, including White Sox pitcher Monty Strat-
ton, *Voyager* co-pilot Jeana Yeager, and World War II hero Audie
Murphy, who enlisted at the old Greenville Post Office.

Location: 600 I-30 E, between exits 95 and 96

Hours: Tuesday - Saturday 10:00 a.m. - 5:00 p.m., Sunday 1:00 -
5:00 p.m.

PUDDIN HILL BAKERY

903-455-6931

Yummmm! You can sniff your way to this scrumptious array of world-famous pecan fruit cakes, chocolate delicacies, and other tempting treats. If you're there at noon, choose from a variety of homemade lunches. Be sure to save room for dessert. Daily tours of the bakery and candy kitchen are available October through December.

Location: I-30 at Division St.

Hours: Monday - Saturday 10:00 a.m. - 5:00 p.m.; open Sundays 1:00 - 5:00 p.m. November - Christmas only

In 1994 cotton was Texas' leading crop with sales of $1.3 billion.

HICO

800-361-HICO
www.hico-tx.com

BILLY THE KID MUSEUM

254-796-4244

According to Hico legend, Billy the Kid wasn't killed by Pat Garrett but died of a heart attack on his way to the post office in Hico at the age of ninety. No matter how Ollie L. "Brushy Bill" Roberts, alias Billy the Kid, died, legends live on. Check out *The Return of the Outlaw Billy the Kid* by W. C. Jameson and Frederick Bean.

Location: Pecan St.

Hours: Friday - Sunday noon - 4:00 p.m.

IRVING

http://www.irvingtexas.com/

DALLAS COWBOYS AND TEXAS STADIUM

972-438-7676
972-554-1804
http://www.dallascowboys.com/

See the home of the five-time Super Bowl champions! Guided stadium tours begin at the Pro Shop located at Gate 8 and include a visit to the exclusive Stadium Club, a private suite, press box, dressing room, and playing field. No tours are given on game day or during special events.

Texas Stadium has:

52 full concession stands
40 speicalty stands
86 restrooms
115 drinking fountains

Location: At the intersection of Texas 183, Texas 114, and Loop 12

Hours: The Pro Shop at the stadium is open Monday - Saturday 9:00 a.m. - 5:00 p.m., Sunday 10:00 a.m. - 4:00 p.m.

MOVIE STUDIOS OF LAS COLINAS

972-869-3456
http://www.studiosatlascolinas.com/enter.html

A must for movie fans, this studio tour gives a glimpse behind the scenes at a working motion picture and television sound stage where such blockbusters as *Silkwood*, *Robocop*, and *JFK* were filmed, as well as the TV series, *Walker, Texas Ranger*. Learn how special effects trick the eye, and discover how makeup and costumes perfect the illusion. See famous costumes including those of Batman, Superman, and Darth Vader and the Storm Troopers in *Star Wars*, as well as Dorothy's blue dress from the *Wizard of Oz*. See sets, including the actual model

submarine used in *The Hunt for Red October*, props, and other movie memorabilia.

The Studio Store is a perfect place to pick up souvenirs from favorite television shows and movies.

Location: 6301 N. O'Connor Rd., Building One

Hours: Open daily; tours at 10:30 a.m., 12:30 p.m., 2:30 p.m., and 4:00 p.m. (no 10:30 a.m. tour on Sunday)

Admission: $12.95/adults, $10.95/seniors 65+, $7.95/children

JACKSBORO

FORT RICHARDSON STATE HISTORIC SITE

http://www.tpwd.state.tx.us/park/parks.htm

This fort was the most northerly of a line of military posts established in Texas after the Civil War to halt plundering and pillage by the Indians. Six original buildings still exist: the morgue, bakery, magazine, commissary, hospital, and part of the guardhouse. A reconstructed officers' barracks serves as the Interpretive Center. Campsites with electricity are available, as are picnic sites, restrooms, showers, nature hiking trails, and a pond for fishing.

Location: Southwest edge of city

Hours: Interpretive Center open daily 8:00 a.m. - 5:00 p.m.

MᴄKɪɴɴᴇʏ

Hᴇᴀʀᴅ Nᴀᴛᴜʀᴀʟ Sᴄɪᴇɴᴄᴇ Mᴜsᴇᴜᴍ ᴀɴᴅ Wɪʟᴅʟɪꜰᴇ Sᴀɴᴄᴛᴜᴀʀʏ

972-542-5566

http://www.heardmuseum.org/

See live animal exhibits along with natural history exhibits of flora, fauna, and geology. This fine museum offers great summer camps and safaris for kids as well as classes and a nice nature store. As you wander trails through the 275-acre wildlife sanctuary, you'll find many scenic picnic areas.

Location: Two miles south on Texas 5, east 1 mile on FM 1378

Hours: Tuesday - Saturday 9:00 a.m. - 5:00 p.m., Sunday 1:00 - 5:00 p.m.

MᴇsQᴜɪᴛᴇ

Cᴇʟᴇʙʀᴀᴛɪᴏɴ Sᴛᴀᴛɪᴏɴ

972-279-7888

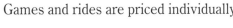

Kids of all ages love the entertaining games, shows, challenging rides, and food court.

Location: 4040 Towne Crossing Blvd.

Hours: Memorial Day - Labor Day: daily 10:00 a.m.; winter: Monday - Thursday 2:00 - 9:00 p.m., Friday 2:00 - midnight, Saturday 10:00 a.m. - midnight, Sunday 11:00 a.m. - 9:00 p.m.

Admission: Games and rides are priced individually

MESQUITE CHAMPIONSHIP RODEO

972-285-8777
http://mesquiterodeo.com/

What a rodeo! This local rodeo has become an extremely popular attraction with coverage on the Nashville Network. Watch calf roping, barrel racing, bull riding, steer wrestling, and bronco riding. Facilities include grandstand seating for 6,500 and a restaurant. Youngsters can enjoy pony rides and the Kiddie Korral.

Location: Near I-635 at Military Parkway

Hours: Performances Friday and Saturday nights April - September

Admission: $8/adults, $10/reserved seats

SAMUELL FARM

972-670-7866

Experience life on a working farm. This 340-acre farm is maintained to re-create farming days of the 1800s to the early 1900s. There's a lot to see and do—ponds for fishing, picnic tables, hayrides, hiking and horse trails, and several animals to pet. Numerous special events are planned throughout the year.

Location: U.S. 80 E, exit Beltline Rd.

Hours: Tuesday - Saturday 9:00 a.m. - 5:00 p.m.

SPECIAL EVENT

MESQUITE HOT AIR BALLOON FESTIVAL

Each July this Hot Air Balloon Festival attracts 250,000 and features balloons from all over the

U.S. as well as aircraft fly overs, parachute jumps, arts and crafts, and musical entertainment.

MEXIA

OLD FORT PARKER STATE HISTORICAL SITE

http://www.tpwd.state.tx.us/park/parks.htm

Nine-year-old Cynthia Ann Parker was captured here in 1836. She grew up, married a Comanche chief, and became the mother of the last great Comanche chief, Quanah Parker. She lived with the Indians until recaptured twenty-four years later in 1860. She never became reconciled to her forced return to the life of the white man and died about four years after she was separated from the wild, free life of the Comanche. The restored fort has pioneer memorabilia, authentic log blockhouses, and a stockade.

Location: Eight miles southwest on Texas 14, Park Road 35

Hours: Daylight Wednesday - Sunday

NORTH RICHLAND HILLS

MOUNTASIA FAMILY FUN CENTER

817-788-0990

Fun for all with Can-Am go-cart track, bumper boat ride, baseball and softball batting cages, and a 36-hole miniature golf

course that takes golfers through caves and waterfalls. The 7,000-square-foot clubhouse includes the latest video games.

Location: 8707 Grapevine Hwy. (Texas 26)

NRH$_2$O FAMILY WATER PARK

817-656-6500
http://www.nrh2o.com/html/start.html

This municipal water park features a fountain entrance and shallow wading stream, children's play area, wave pool, 600-linear-foot "endless river," water slides, sand volleyball court, arcade, gift shop, and concessions. The exciting six-story "Master Blaster" uphill water coaster was added in 1998.

Location: 9001 Grapevine Hwy (Texas 26)

Hours: Summer: Sunday - Thursday 10:00 a.m. - 8:00 p.m., Friday and Saturday 10:00 a.m. - 10:00 p.m.

Admission: $12.95/adults, $10.95/children ages 3-11, free for children under 3

PARKS

Of the five city parks, the most exceptional one is Adventure World Park, a 10-acre fully handicapped accessible facility. The playground offers recreational play while teaching skills to children. Ride a mock train and helicopter or work out in the fitness section with sit-up and pull-up bars and other equipment.

Location: Adventure World - Starnes Rd. between Holiday and Douglas Lanes

PLANO

Plano Convention & Visitors Bureau
800-81-PLANO
http://www.tourtexas.com/plano/plano.html

PARKS

972-461-7250

An award-winning park system includes over 3,300 acres of public parks throughout the city. Facilities include indoor and outdoor swimming pools, four recreation centers, 79 tennis courts, 3 municipal golf courses, 74 soccer/football fields, 49 baseball fields, an outdoor learning center, playground for handicapped children, and 30 miles of hike-and-bike trails.

SOUTHFORK RANCH

800-989-7800 or 972-442-7800

Made famous by the *Dallas* TV series, the home of the infamous Ewing clan is now open for tours. View the opulent mansion and sprawling grounds and see the gun that shot J.R., Lucy's wedding dress, and other memorabilia from the show.

Location: 3700 Hogge Rd.—take U.S. 75 North, exit 30, east on FM 2514/Parker Rd. about six miles; right on FM 2551/Hogge Rd.

Hours: Daily 9:00 a.m. - 6:00 p.m.

Admission: Free admission to ranch; tours: $6.95/adults, $5.95/seniors, $4.95/children 4-12, children under 4 free

SPECIAL EVENT

PLANO BALLOON FESTIVAL
972-867-7566

Each September this Balloon Festival is a spectacular three-day event that offers something for everyone—an arts and crafts fair, continuous stage entertainment, and a kids art tent, in addition to the spectacular hot air balloons.

Location: Bob Woodruff Park, 2601 San Gabriel

Admission: FREE

SALADO

http://www.salado.com/

PACE PARK AND SALADO CREEK

Picnic beside picturesque Salado Creek, Texas' first designated natural landmark. The site was an Indian campground long before recorded history. Since Main Street was part of the Chisholm Trail, ruts from wagon wheels still appear in the bedrock of the creek just north of the park.

TEAGUE

BURLINGTON-ROCK ISLAND RAILROAD MUSEUM

The first streamlined passenger train in Texas, the "Sam Houston Zephyr," was inaugurated in 1936 between Dallas-Fort Worth and Houston. The old two-story 1906 brick depot is listed on the National Register of Historic Places and is now a museum with relics and mementos from the golden age of railroads. Also on site is a log home, complete with period furnishings, built in the early 1850s.

Location: 208 S. Third Ave.

Hours: Saturday and Sunday 1:00 - 5:00 p.m.

TEMPLE

RAILROAD AND PIONEER MUSEUM

254-298-5172

Housed in a restored vintage depot, exhibits are devoted to pioneer farming and ranching and the early days of railroading in Texas.

Location: S. 31st and Ave. H

Hours: Tuesday - Friday 1:00 - 4:00 p.m., Saturday 10:00 a.m. - 4:00 p.m.

TERRELL

SILENT WINGS MUSEUM

This museum pays tribute to a little-known part of Texas history. It's dedicated to the airborne personnel of WW II with a special emphasis on the momentous role of glider pilots. Watch the fascinating tapes of gliders in action as well as viewing the exhibits of memorabilia and weapons from the WW II era.

Location: Municipal airport, two miles north of I-20 via Texas 34 (exit 501) and Airport Rd.

Hours: Tuesday - Saturday 10:00 a.m. - 5:00 p.m., Sunday noon - 5:00 p.m.

Admission: FREE

WACO

Convention & Visitors Bureau Visitor Center
University Parks Dr. off I-35, exit 335B
800-WACO-FUN (922-6386) or 254-750-8696
http://www.wacocvb.com/

BRAZOS TROLLEY

The air-conditioned trolley stops at most of Waco's attractions and provides a great way for tourists and campers to park their vehicles and see the sights. The Brazos Trolley stops at the Texas Ranger Museum, Dr Pepper Museum, Indian Spring Park/Suspension Bridge, East Terrace House, Cameron Park Zoo, Earle-Harrison House, Waco Convention Center, East Bank Area, and Texas Sports Hall of Fame.

Location: Tourist Information Center in Fort Fisher Park

Hours: Summer: daily; weekends only September - November and March - May. Trolleys run approximately every 20 minutes on Saturdays, and about every 35 to 45 minutes on weekdays and Sundays. Pick up a schedule at the Tourist Info Center for more detail.

Admission: 50¢/adults, 25¢/seniors and students, children 5 and under ride FREE with an adult. Transfers are free. Please have exact change ready, drivers do not carry money and are unable to make change.

CAMERON PARK ZOO

254-750-8400
http://www.waco-texas.com/lev2.cfm/15

Kids always have fun at the Cameron Park Zoo! This 51-acre natural habitat zoo sits near the Brazos River amid pecan, elm, live oak, burr oak, cottonwood, and mesquite trees. Recreational as well as educational, it emphasizes conservation by participating in the Species Survival Plan and by housing many endangered or threatened species. It is home for gibbon apes, Sumatran tigers, white rhinos, giraffes, zebras, antelopes, and many others. See Gibbon Island and African Treetops Village. Special events throughout the year include Kids Zoobilee, week-long and day camps, and one-day educational programs.

Don't leave before you enjoy Cameron Park itself. Slide through tunnels and swing or hang like a monkey. Stroll through Miss Nellie's Pretty Place, a wildflower preserve that's as pretty as a picture from March through June. Hike or ride a bike on the easy, scenic nature trail that follows the river and takes you past ancient cliffs where sea creatures lived 100 million years ago. Go to the top of the cliffs and look out over the Brazos River and beyond.

Location: 1701 N. Fourth St.

Hours: Monday - Saturday 9:00 a.m. - 5:00 p.m., Sunday 11:00 a.m. - 5:00 p.m. (until 6:00 p.m. during summer); closed New Year's Day, Thanksgiving, and Christmas

Admission: $4/adults, $2/children

DR PEPPER MUSEUM

254-757-1024
http://www.drpeppermuseum.com/

A fountain drink mixed in the Old Corner Drug Store in the 1880s was dubbed a "Waco" by early patrons because Waco was the only place it could be found. Now known as Dr Pepper, the new drink was put on sale commercially in 1885, after two years of testing, blending, and processing. The formula has remained basically unchanged.

The museum is housed in the original 1906 bottling plant, now listed on the National Register of Historic Places. The first floor has a replica of the drug store where Dr Pepper was invented, complete with an animatron of pharmacist Charles Curtis Alderton telling of his invention.

Location: 300 S. Fifth St.

Hours: Monday - Saturday 10:00 a.m. - 4:00 p.m., Sunday noon - 4:00 p.m.

Admission: $4/adults, $2/children

GOVERNOR BILL AND VERA DANIEL HISTORIC VILLAGE

254-755-1160

This turn-of-the-century Texas village has been carefully moved to thirteen acres along the Brazos River. Twenty preserved and

restored buildings portray life in early Texas. See a planter's home as well as sharecropper houses, a hotel, church, saloon, cotton gin, and a blacksmith shop.

Location: 1108 University Parks Dr.

Hours: Tuesday - Friday 10:00 a.m. - 4:00 p.m., Saturday and Sunday 1:00 - 5:00 p.m.

Admission: $3/adults, $2/seniors, $1/students

Strecker Museum

254-755-1110

The Strecker Museum claims to be the oldest continuously operated museum in Texas. Almost 150 years of collecting has produced extensive geological, biological, and anthropological artifacts and an excellent look at Indian life and lore.

Location: Sid Richardson Hall on Baylor University Campus

Hours: Tuesday - Friday 9:00 a.m. - noon, 1:30 - 4:00 p.m., Saturday 10:00 a.m. - noon, 1:30 - 4:00 p.m., Sunday 2:00 - 5:00 p.m.; closed holidays

Admission: FREE

Texas Ranger Hall of Fame and Museum at Fort Fisher

254-750-8631
http://www.texasranger.org/

Few heroes from history books have ever captured our imagination as much as the notorious Texas Rangers. This hall of fame and museum complex commemorates the history and lore of the legendary Texas Rangers, the oldest state law enforcement agency in the nation. See treasured collections of guns and weapons from the Old West, Texas Ranger badges, a Bowie knife owned by Jim Bowie, and the weapons and possessions of Bonnie and Clyde.

The Moody Texas Ranger Memorial Library contains books, archives, photographs, and oral histories related to the Texas Rangers.

You can purchase a piece of the legend—officially licensed souvenirs are available at the museum store. It has an exceptional selection of books, too.

Fort Fisher Park is a scenic 35 acres along Lake Brazos, near the site of the original Texas Ranger fort established in 1837. Shaded riverside campsites, RV and picnic sites are available.

Location: I-35 at University Parks Dr.

Hours: Museum: Daily 9:00 a.m. - 5:00 p.m., closed New Year's Day, Thanksgiving, and Christmas

Admission: $3.75/adult, $1.75/children 6 -12, children under 5 free

TEXAS SPORTS HALL OF FAME

254-756-1633

The Texas Sports Hall of Fame is a tribute to the pursuit of excellence and a showcase of legendary greats. Sports memorabilia highlight nationally known Texans, including Byron Nelson, Lee Trevino, Babe Didrikson Zaharias, George Foreman, and Nolan Ryan, to name a few. See the 1938 Heisman Trophy presented to TCU quarterback Davey O'Brien, and game jerseys worn by Bob Lilly and Roger Staubach. Watch videos of historic sports events in the Tom Landry Theater. Visit the Texas Baseball Hall of Fame, Tennis Hall of Fame, and the Texas High School Halls of Fame for football, basketball, and baseball.

Location: 1108 S. University Parks Dr., next to Fort Fisher Park

Hours: Monday - Saturday 10:00 a.m. - 5:00 p.m., Sunday noon - 5:00 p.m.

Admission: $4/adults, $3.50/seniors and students

WACO SUSPENSION BRIDGE

Built in 1870, Waco's historic suspension bridge provided cattle and cowboys following the Chisholm Trail the only pedestrian/wagon span across the Brazos River. Completed in January of 1870, the 475-foot bridge required 2,700,000 bricks and cost $135,000 to build. Designed by the renowned New York firm that originated the suspension span bridge concept and later oversaw the building of the Brooklyn Bridge, it was the longest single-span suspension bridge west of the Mississippi at the time.

WAGON TOURS

"The World Famous James S. Wood" offers a mule-drawn wagon tour of Waco, complete with "more lies and stories about Waco than you ever heard." This former alligator wrestler serves as Waco's ambassador to hundreds of tourists who take his tour each year.

Location: Tours departs from the Texas Ranger Museum (see above).

Hours: May - October Monday - Friday 10:00 a.m. - 3:30 p.m., weather permitting

Admission: $6/adults, $3/children

WAXAHACHIE

Waxahachie Convention and Visitors Bureau
102 YMCA Drive
972-937-2390

ELLIS COUNTY COURTHOUSE

This elaborate structure of red sandstone and granite was built
in 1895 for the then-outlandish cost of $150,000. Artisans were
brought from Italy to do the exterior stone carving. The clock
uses a windup mechanism that weighs 250 pounds and the bell-
striker weighs over 800 pounds.

CATFISH PLANTATION

972-937-9468

This famous "haunted restaurant" has three
friendly resident ghosts, first-rate catfish, and
great Cajun food. Ghostly experiences don't
occur on a daily basis, but there's always someone around to tell you tales of prior incidents.

Location: 814 Water St.

Hours: Open Thursday - Sunday

SPECIAL EVENT

SCARBOROUGH FAIRE

http://www.iitexas.com/gpages/faire1.htm

Enter a time machine! Return to the sixteenth century for a day
of fun and frivolity. This springtime Renaissance fair features
over two hundred permanent craft shops, food booths, and

medieval entertainment—wizards, jugglers, jesters, and puppet shows, costumes of royalty, and rascals, poets, and peasants.

Location: In rural setting on FM 66, 1.6 miles west of I-35 E

Hours: Eight weekends mid-April through early June

WICHITA FALLS

Convention & Visitors Bureau
1000 Fifth St.
940-716-5500
http://www.wf.net/~mpec/

PARKS

Throughout the city, thirty-eight parks offer outdoor recreation, swimming pools, jogging trails, golf, tennis, picnicking, and children's fishing ponds. Lucy Park is a 170-acre park with a restored log cabin, pool, Lucy Land playground, duck pond, paved trail, pavilions, picnicking areas, and restrooms. A river walk trail along the Wichita River connects Lucy Park to the Wichita Falls Waterfall, a re-creation of the original falls that washed away in a flood in 1886.

PLEX ENTERTAINMENT CENTER

940-696-1222

Fun for all with go-carts, bumper boats, video arcade, two 18-hole miniature golf courses, and more.

Location: 4131 Southwest Parkway

Hours: Sunday - Thursday 11:00 a.m. - 10:00 p.m., Friday 11:00 a.m. - midnight, Saturday 10:00 a.m. - midnight

North East

ALTO

CADDOAN INDIAN MOUNDS

800-792-1112

One of the main archaeological sites in Texas, this park includes a full-size replica of a Caddoan house built with Stone Age-type tools, visitor center with exhibits, and an interpretive trail. Two ceremonial mounds are remains of ancient Indian culture.

Location: Six miles southwest of Alto on Texas 21

Hours: Friday - Monday 9:00 a.m. - 6:00 p.m.; closed major holidays

ATHENS

Visitor Initiative Program
100 W. Tyler St.
888-294-2847 or 903-677-0775

ATHENS SCUBA PARK AND AQUANAUT DIVING

903-675-5762

Divers flock to this 7½-acre clear blue lake (no boats permitted) for recreational diving and for diver certification. Eleven docks have training platforms, and the dive shop rents gear if you don't have your own. There are also basketball courts, volleyball, and thirty acres of paintball.

Location: 500 N. Murchison St.

Hours: Summer: Wednesday - Sunday 9:00 a.m. - dark; winter: Saturday and Sunday 10:00 a.m. - dark

TEXAS FRESHWATER FISHERIES CENTER

903-676-2277

This innovative complex features over 300,000 gallons of aquarium exhibits, and visitors can see nearly every major species of freshwater fish found in Texas in its natural habitat. Explore the Hill Country stream, East Texas farm pond, or go below the surface of a Texas reservoir. Gaze into the eyes of an American alligator in a natural wetland environment. Wander through a variety of showcases that feature replicas of most state record fish caught in Texas freshwater lakes and streams. Watch and even talk to divers as they hand-feed the largest largemouth bass in captivity in a 26,000 gallon dive tank. Go to the angler's pavilion and casting pond for a hands-on experience catching rainbow trout or channel catfish.

Location: 5550 Flat Creek Rd. (FM 2495) near Lake Athens

Hours: Tuesday - Saturday 9:00 a.m. - 4:00 p.m., Sunday 1: 00 - 4:00 p.m.; closed New Year's Day, Easter Sunday, Thanksgiving, Christmas Eve, and Christmas Day

 ## SPECIAL EVENTS

OLD FIDDLERS REUNION has been held for over fifty-five years on the last Friday in May. There's fiddlin' for all ages, a street dance, and carnival.

BLACK-EYED PEA JAMBOREE, held the third weekend in July, features a cook-off, arts and crafts show, carnival, races, and pea poppin' and pea shellin' contests.

> In the 1880s Fletcher Davis invented a popular sandwich, a ground beef patty served between two slices of bread with mustard and a slice of onion, and served it at a lunch counter on the courthouse square. "Uncle Fletch" took it to the 1904 World's Fair in St. Louis and the rest is history.

UNCLE FLETCH'S HAMBURGER COOKOFF is held the fourth Saturday in September to commemorate this famous invention.

BONHAM

Bonham Area Chamber of Commerce
110 E. First St.
903-583-4811
http://www.netexas.net/bacc/

BONHAM STATE PARK

http://www.tpwd.state.tx.us/park/parks.htm

This scenic 300-acre park sits on a rolling, wooded site less than four miles from Bonham. There are camping facilities, and a small lake offers fishing, swimming, and boating. Other facilities include a bathhouse, snack bar (summer), miniature golf course, playground, and pedal-boat rentals.

Location: Texas 78 south, FM 271

FORT INGLISH PARK

903-583-3441

This historic park features a replica of a log blockhouse and stockade built in 1837 and the nucleus of homesteads that became the town of Bonham—three restored log cabins, pioneer furnishings, and artifacts.

Location: W. Sam Rayburn Dr.

Hours: April 1 - September 1: Tuesday - Friday 10:00 a.m. - 4:00 p.m., Saturday and Sunday 1:00 - 5:00 p.m.

CADDO LAKE

see: UNCERTAIN

CARTHAGE

JIM REEVES MEMORIAL

A life-sized statue of Jim Reeves commemorates the Panola County native who became one of America's best-loved country-western singers. A member of the Country Music Hall of Fame, with millions of records to his credit, he died in a plane crash in 1964.

Location: Three miles east of downtown on US 79

TEX RITTER MUSEUM

903-693-6634

The museum is dedicated to this legendary country-western entertainer who was an early member of the Grand Ol' Opry and the Country Music Hall of Fame.

Location: 300 W. Panola

Hours: Monday - Friday 8:30a.m. - 4:30 p.m., Saturday 1:00 - 4:00 p.m.

CROCKETT

Davy Crockett stopped here to camp on his way to the Alamo! Or so legend has it. The city was named for the famous frontiersman who died at the Alamo. It's among the oldest towns in Texas and the site of many historic structures.

DAVY CROCKETT MEMORIAL PARK

This park has picnic areas, tennis courts, playgrounds, pavilion and civic buildings, and an adjacent swimming pool and athletic stadium.

DAVY CROCKETT SPRING

According to legend, this was the campsite of Col. Davy Crockett and a small detachment of men on their way to San Antonio to help defend the Alamo. A historical plaque marks the site where the spring still flows.

Location: W. Goliad Street at the underpass

GRAND SALINE

Grand Saline Chamber of Commerce
903-962-5631

SALT PALACE

903-962-5631

Don't lick the building! A building made out of SALT? Since Grand Saline is the location of a huge underground salt mine, a Salt Palace was built for the Texas Centennial in 1936. The one you'll see today was built in 1993 and is the third since the

original—they melt away after a few years. It now serves as an information center and museum where visitors can see a film showing a tour inside a salt mine, and exhibits of salt mine memorabilia and salt-related items.

Location: U.S. 80 at Main Street

Hours: Tuesday - Saturday 8:30 a.m. - 5:00 p.m.

HENDERSON

Rusk County Chamber of Commerce
201 North Main
903-657-5528
http://www.hendersontx.com/

DEPOT MUSEUM AND CHILDREN'S DISCOVERY CENTER

903-657-4303

This restored 1901 Missouri Pacific Railroad depot houses a museum of Rusk County history in the old waiting room. The warehouse portion of the depot is a hands-on learning center for children ages three to eleven. On the grounds is a restored 1908 "Arnold Outhouse," the first outhouse in the state to receive a historical marker. The ornate, gingerbread-style three-holer was built for a prominent turn-of-the-century attorney.

Location: 514 N. High Street

Hours: Monday - Friday 9:00 a.m. - 5:00 p.m., Saturday 9:00 a.m. - 1:00 p.m.

Admission: $2/adult, $1/children under 12

JACKSONVILLE

Jacksonville Chamber of Commerce
903-586-2217

JACKSONVILLE CANDY COMPANY

903-586-8334

This family-owned candy company has long been famous for its peanut brittle, peanut logs, and peanut patties. Watch how the candy is made, then stock up on delicious treats by the sample, the box, or the pound.

Location: 218 Woodrow

Hours: Monday - Thursday 8:00 a.m. - 5:00 p.m., Fri. 8:00 a.m. - 4:00 p.m.

TEXAS BASKET COMPANY

903-586-8014

This is one of only three basket makers still in operation in the U.S. You can watch the basket making process from a viewing platform. The Texas Basket Company began production in 1924 and still uses the original equipment to process the wood and make baskets. The wood they use is cut within 200 miles of Jacksonville. A well-stocked gift shop sells all kinds of baskets (even "seconds"), as well as country crafts, gift items, books, and toys. Partially wheelchair accessible.

Location: 100 Myrtle Dr.

Hours: Monday - Saturday 8:00 a.m. - 5:00 p.m. Group tours of factory and store available.

Admission: FREE

JEFFERSON

Marion County Chamber of Commerce
116 W. Austin
903-665-2672
http://jeffersontx.com/jefferson/

Visit the era when Jefferson was once a major Texas river port.
Tour a Victorian home, take a boat tour of Cypress Bayou, and
ride through town on a trolley tour or horse-drawn carriage. The
history of this quaint little town is evident everywhere.

CADDO LAKE—see: UNCERTAIN

CARNEGIE LIBRARY

Built in 1907, this is one of only a few remaining
Carnegie libraries still serving its original purpose. One of the most outstanding doll
collections in Texas is on display here.

Location: 301 Lafayette St.

Hours: Tuesday - Friday 12:00 noon - 5:00 p.m., Saturday 9:00
a.m. - 1:00 p.m.

JEFFERSON GENERAL STORE AND OLD-FASHIONED SODA FOUNTAIN

How long since you've been to a real old-fashioned soda fountain? Here's one that features Blue Bell ice cream and nickel
coffee. Treat yourself to a soda, shake, or float while you browse
the Texas souvenirs and merchandise. Ask to see the old juke-
boxes and soda machines.

Location: 113 E. Austin

TOURS

Information and tickets for these and other Jefferson and Caddo Lake tours are available at Tour Headquarters, 222 E. Austin, 903-665-1665.

- Bayou Riding Stables —A 45-minute narrated horseback tour amid century-old trees along the banks of Cypress Bayou. 903-665-7600

- Caddo Lake Steamboat Company—Narrated 1½-hour paddle wheel riverboat tours of scenic Caddo Lake. 888-325-5459 or 903-789-3978

- City Trolley Tours—Narrated tours tell the history of Jefferson while passing points of interest. Trolley departs daily from Historic Jefferson Tour Headquarters at 222 E. Austin St. 903-665-1665

- Mule-Drawn Wagon Tours—For some 25 years open-air wagons have offered narrated tours of Jefferson. Board across from museum in the Riverfront District.

- Mullins Carriage Service—903-665-2857 or 903-665-1874

- Romantic Carriage Service—Narrated city tours. 903-668-3318

- Turning Basin Boat Tours—Take a one-hour narrated tour of Cypress Bayou to learn some history, enjoy nature, and have some fun. Located at the riverfront, across the bridge from historic downtown. 903-665-2222

EXCELSIOR HOUSE

903-665-2513

This wonderful old hotel has been in continuous operation since it was built in the 1850s. Restored to its former grandeur, it features French chandeliers, Oriental rugs, and marble

mantels. The Excelsior's Plantation breakfasts feature its famous orange blossom muffins.

Location: 211 W. Austin.

JEFFERSON HOTEL

903-665-2631

If you want to stay in a haunted hotel, this is the place! The hotel has quite a checkered and colorful past. It was "the" place to be during the great steamboat era and has now been restored to much of its original Victorian charm. The staff will share the ghostly legends if you wish.

Location: 124 W. Austin

KILGORE

Kilgore Chamber of Commerce
903-984-5022
http://www.ci.kilgore.tx.us/home/

EAST TEXAS OIL MUSEUM

903-983-8295

Dioramas, films, sounds, and mementos of the oil field re-create the oil boom days of the 1930s. A vintage drilling rig is displayed outside. Ride a simulated 3,800-foot elevator to the oil formations within the earth.

Location: On the campus of Kilgore College, U.S. 259 at Ross St.

Hours: Tuesday - Saturday 9:00 a.m. - 4:00 p.m., Sunday 2:00 - 5:00 p.m.; special holiday schedule between Christmas and New Year's Day

Admission: $4/adults, $2/children 3-11

RANGERETTE SHOWCASE

903-983-8265

The Kilgore College Rangerettes' performances at bowl and international games has brought fame to Kilgore College. The first of its kind, this world-famous precision drill and dance team was formed in 1940 as halftime entertainment for local football games. This museum features films and displays of props, costumes, uniforms, awards, and mementos.

Location: On the college campus

Hours: Monday - Friday 9:00 a.m.- noon, 1:00 - 5:00 p.m., Saturday 10:00 a.m. - noon, 1:00 - 4:00 p.m.; special holiday schedule between Christmas and New Year's Day.

Admission: FREE

WORLD'S RICHEST ACRE PARK

The greatest concentration of oil wells in the world once stood on part of one downtown block. One original derrick and twelve new ones, a restored pumpjack, and a granite monument to the pioneer oil families of East Texas are a tribute to the great oil boom of the 1930s.

Location: Main and Commerce St., across from the railroad depot

LONGVIEW

Longview Convention & Visitors Bureau
410 N. Center St.
903-753-3281
http://www.longviewtx.com

PLANTATION POTTERY

903-663-3387

See potters turning their wares on Fridays and Saturdays. This enormous facility is a 57,000-square-foot complex on ten landscaped acres. It includes a 10,000-square-foot greenhouse, "miniature world" (an Old West village on miniature scale), and nature trails. Fun for all.

Location: From I-20 take Eastman Rd. exit, then north on U.S. 259 for 6.5 miles.

Hours: Monday - Saturday 10:00 a.m. - 8:00 p.m., Sunday 12:30 - 6:00 p.m.

SPECIAL EVENT

GREAT TEXAS BALLOON RACE is an annual three-day hot air balloon festival located at Gregg County Airport each July. Balloonists and spectators come from around the country.

LUFKIN

Lufkin Visitor & Convention Bureau
409-634-6305
http://www.chamber.angelina.tx.us/tourinfo.htm

ELLEN TROUT ZOO AND PARK

409-633-0399

This fully accredited zoo displays a wide variety of animals and birds and is well known for its breeding programs for West African crowned cranes and Louisiana pine snakes.

Location: 402 Zoo Circle off Loop 287 North

Hours: Daily 9:00 a.m. - 5:00 p.m.; until 6:00 p.m. in summer

Admission: $2/ages 12 and up, $1/ages 4-12, 3 and under free

TEXAS FORESTRY MUSEUM

409-632-9535

See early logging machinery, wildland fire fighting equipment and fire tower, an old railroad depot, and antique railroad and sawmill steam engines at this unusual museum. Other exhibits include forestlands flora and fauna, a mini-woodland trail, and an old sawmill town.

Location: 1905 Atkinson Dr.

Hours: Monday - Saturday 10:00 a.m. - 5:00 p.m., Sunday 1:00 - 5:00 p.m.; closed major holidays

MARSHALL

Greater Marshall Chamber of Commerce
213 W. Austin
903-935-7868
http://www.marshalltxchamber.com

MARSHALL POTTERY'S OLD WORLD STORE AND MUSEUM

903-938-9201

Everyone will enjoy a visit to one of the largest manufacturers of glazed pottery in the U.S. Established in 1896, it produces millions of red clay and hand-turned stoneware pots yearly. The museum shows the art form of pottery with a video presentation that takes visitors through the entire process from digging the clay to making the finished pieces. At the main showroom, visitors will see hundreds of kinds of pottery items and regular demonstrations of pottery making and firing.

Location: 2.5 miles southeast of Marshall on FM 31

Hours: Monday - Saturday 9:00 a.m. - 8:00 p.m., Sunday 10:00 a.m. - 6:00 p.m.

T.C. LINDSEY AND CO.

903-687-3382

Calling all nostalgia buffs! This part-museum, part-authentic 1880s general store offers a wide variety of merchandise as well as a visit to nostalgialand. The fascinating store has so much character that it has been used in several Disney films.

Location: In tiny Jonesville, two miles west of the Louisiana state line and two miles north of U.S. 80 on FM 134

161

Hours: Tuesday-Saturday 8:00 a.m. - 4:00 p.m.

SPECIAL EVENT

 ### WONDERLAND OF LIGHTS

Described as "totally amazing" and "unbelievable" by visitors from around the world, this
annual festival is one of the largest concerted
holiday light shows in the U.S. Millions of tiny white lights illu-
minate the city. Hundreds of businesses outline buildings and
decorate windows; entire neighborhoods decorate; more than
125,000 lights decorate the historic Courthouse Museum.
Thanksgiving through New Year's Day.

MINEOLA

Chamber of Commerce
101 E. Broad
800-MINEOLA or 903-569-2087
http://www.easttexas.com/mineola

KITCHEN'S HARDWARE AND DELI

No one should pass through Mineola without a stop at Kitchen's.
The deli serves great sandwiches, salads, and soups made fresh
with locally produced ingredients. Their peppered bacon has
become so famous it's sold by mail order around
the country. The hardware store is a trip back in
time, from the pot-bellied stove to the 1903
hand-operated Otis rope elevator in the back.
Shelves groan with items your children have
never seen.

Location: 119 E. Broad

NACOGDOCHES

Convention & Visitors Bureau
513 North St.
888-564-7351 or 409-564-7351
www.visitnacogdoches.org

This town, one of the oldest in Texas, is a major attraction for
history buffs, who come to see the Oak Grove Cemetery, Old
Nacogdoches University, Old North Church, Old Stone Fort,
Sterne-Hoya Home, El Camino Real, and other remnants of the
past.

MILLARD'S CROSSING

409-564-6631

See a "village" of restored nineteenth-century buildings furnished with antiques and pioneer memorabilia.

Location: 6020 North St. (U.S. 59 north)

Hours: Guided tours Monday - Saturday 9:00 a.m. - 4:00 p.m.,
Sunday 1:00 - 4:00 p.m.

Admission: $3/adult, $2/children under 12

STONE FORT MUSEUM

409-468-2408

View artifacts that have been uncovered during the excavation of
a nearby Caddo Indian burial ground. Built in 1779, the fort has
served over the years as a trading post, jail, courthouse, and
capitol, as well as headquarters for four different attempts to
establish the Republic of Texas. Now a museum, the Stone Fort
Museum also contains restored period rooms and exhibits of
early East Texas. Partially wheelchair accessible.

Location: Griffith and Clark St. on the campus of Stephen F. Austin State University

Hours: Tuesday - Saturday 9:00 a.m. - 5:00 p.m., Sun. 1:00 - 5:00 p.m.

Admission: FREE

PALESTINE

Visitor Center (Chamber of Commerce)
In historic 1914 Carnegie Library
502 N. Queen at Crawford St.
903-729-6066

DAVEY DOGWOOD PARK
903-729-7275

 This is an exceptionally beautiful park, especially from late March and early April during the annual Texas Dogwood Trails. Paved roads wind through the 200-acre park of rolling hills, clear flowing streams, forests, and meadows. Call for information on the Dogwood Trails.

Location: Just north of Palestine on N. Link St.

TEXAS STATE RAILROAD STATE HISTORICAL PARK—see also: RUSK
800/442-8951 (in Texas) or
903/683-2561
http://www.tpwd.state.tx.us/park/parks.
htm

164

Antique steam engines travel the 25½-mile route to Rusk through dense East Texas forests. The huge locomotive #610 that was restored to pull the Bicentennial Freedom Train in Texas in 1976 is on exhibit. See an 1899 wooden T & P business car and an old baggage car; tour the steam engine cab and visit the engineer. An "O" gauge model train room with over 800 feet of track is also open. On selected weekends each month, the park offers steam engine shop tours, tours of the 1927 Texas & Pacific 610 steam engine, and train seminars and workshops. Call for dates and times.

Location: The terminal, built to resemble a turn-of-the-century depot, is on U.S. 84, three miles east of Palestine.

Hours: Thursday - Sunday June and July; weekends only March - May and August - October; reservations advisable

Train Fares: adult round-trip $15, child (3-12) round-trip $9; adult one-way $10, child (3-12) one-way $6, children under 3 free

PARIS

Chamber of Commerce
800-727-4789
http://www.paristexas.com/

See the "Second Largest Eiffel Tower in the Second Largest Paris." Next to the Love Civic Center at Jefferson Rd. and S. Collegiate Dr., this Eiffel Tower stands slightly over 65 feet tall and represents a remarkable community effort.

PITTSBURG

Pittsburg Chamber of Commerce
109 Forest Hills
903-856-3442

EZEKIEL AIRSHIP

In 1902 a colorful preacher-inventor built a flying machine supposedly based on a description in the Bible book of Ezekiel. Many Pittsburg residents say it flew briefly, but the machine was destroyed in a rail accident on the way to St. Louis World's Fair in 1904. There's a historical marker at the Pittsburg Foundry, the original building site. A full-size replica of the flying machine is displayed in Warrick's restaurant in downtown Pittsburg.

RUSK

TEXAS STATE RAILROAD STATE HISTORICAL PARK—see also: PALESTINE

P O Box 39
Rusk TX 75785
800/442-8951 (in Texas) or 903/683-2561
http://www.tpwd.state.tx.us/park/parks.htm

Antique steam engines travel the 25½-mile route to Palestine through dense East Texas forests.

> The Texas State Railroad State Historic Park contains 110 acres, 30 miles of track, and 24 bridges. The longest bridge spans 110 feet across the Neches River.

166

Location: The Terminal, built to resemble a turn-of-the-century depot, is at the State Park three miles west of downtown Rusk on U.S. 84.

Hours: Thursday - Sunday June and July; weekends only March - May and August - October; reservations advisable

Train Fares: adult round-trip $15, child (3-12) round-trip $9; adult one-way $10, child (3-12) one-way $6, children under 3 free

Texas State Railroad
Photo courtesy of Texas State Railroad State Historic Park, photo by Paul Hausman

167

SULPHUR SPRINGS

Tourism & Visitors Bureau
888-300-6623
http://www.tourtexas.com/sulphursprings

SOUTHWEST DAIRY CENTER AND MUSEUM

903-439-MILK (6455)
http://www.geocities.com/Heartland/Ranch/3541/

When you see the enormous white native stone barn, complete with silo, you've found a very unusual museum. It tells the story of the dairy industry and farm life using pliable mannequins in scenes and exhibits. There's also an old-time soda fountain serving malts, milk shakes, and sundaes and a general store offering unique dairy-related items and souvenirs.

Location: 1200 Houston St.

Hours: Monday - Saturday 9:00 a.m. - 5:00 p.m.

Admission: FREE

ST. CLAIR MUSIC BOX GALLERY

903-885-4926

Girls of all ages will love this amazing collection, one of the largest collections of its kind in the world. Started with a gift from the Queen of Belgium in 1919, the collection now has more than 150 music boxes.

Location: Displayed in the library at 201 N. Davis St.

Hours: Monday - Friday 9:00 a.m. - 6:00 p.m., Saturday 9:00 a.m. - noon

168

Sulphur Springs City Park

This lovely city park is a place for kids to play on the playground, feed the ducks and geese on the lake, and picnic under the trees.

Location: At the intersection of Connally and League Streets

Texarkana

Texarkana Chamber of Commerce
819 State Line
903-792-7191

Crystal Springs Beach

This family-oriented theme park is centered around a twelve-acre spring-fed lake. Activities include a video arcade, concessions, picnic area, and camping facilities with hookups.

Location: 18 miles west on U.S. 67

Hours: Daily Memorial Day - Labor Day; weekends in May

The Discovery Place

903-794-3466

See rotating displays for children, hands-on exhibits, and audio-visual presentations.

Location: 215 Pine St.

Hours: Tuesday - Saturday 10:00 a.m. - 4:00 p.m.

OAKLAWN OPRY

903-838-3333

Oaklawn Opry offers good ol' family entertainment every Saturday night with country-western music.

Location: In Oaklawn Village at Robison Rd. and New Boston Rd.

Hours: Doors open at 6:30, show starts at 7:30

TEXARKANA FUN PARK

See life-sized replicas of wildlife animals and enjoy go-carts and miniature golf.

Location: Three miles north of I-30 on North State Line Rd.

Hours: Monday - Thursday 10:00 a.m. - 10:30p.m., Friday - Saturday 10:00 a.m. - 11:30p.m., Sun 1:00 - 10:30 p.m.

TYLER

Tyler Convention & Visitors Bureau
800-235-5712 or 903-592-1661
www.tylertexas.com

BROOKSHIRE'S WORLD OF WILDLIFE MUSEUM AND COUNTRY STORE

903-534-2169

Go on an African safari right here in Tyler. This museum displays more than 250 specimens of animals, reptiles, and fish from Africa and North America. The Country Store gives you a glimpse into a 1928 grocery store. There's also a 1926 Model T

Ford delivery truck and an old-time gasoline pump. Outside is an antique fire truck and picnic tables.

Location: WSW Loop 323 and Old Jacksonville Hwy.

Hours: Tuesday - Saturday 9:00 a.m. - noon and 1:00 - 5:00 p.m.; closed major holidays

Admission: FREE

CALDWELL ZOO

This fine zoo is designed especially for children and includes a petting zoo. It started in 1938 as a backyard menagerie and is now a 35-acre zoo complete with elephant and giraffe houses, a monkey island, birds, bears, alligators, a native Texas exhibit, and even a cow (milking hours posted).

Location: 2203 Martin Luther King Dr.

Hours: Daily April - September: 9:30 a.m. - 6:00 p.m.; October - March: 9:30 a.m. - 4:30 p.m.

Admission: FREE

DISCOVERY SCIENCE PLACE

903-533-1066
http://tyler.iamerica.net/discovery/

This hands-on children's learning center makes learning fun with exhibits in two large halls. Star in your own live performance on KIDS-TV.

Location: 308 N. Broadway

Hours: Memorial Day - Labor Day: Monday - Saturday 9:00 a.m. - 5:00 p.m.; Labor Day - Memorial Day: Tuesday - Saturday 9:00 a.m. - 5:00 p.m.

Admission: $3.50 for one exhibit or $5 for both, children 2 and under are free; senior discount

FIRE MOUNTAIN AMUSEMENT PARK

903-561-2670

Fire Mountain has a tremendous variety of activities for family fun. The park is designed so families can play together. Little ones and adults can ride the boats and two-seater go-carts together, and the 18-hole miniature golf course is a challenge for all. Toddlers receive a complimentary club so they can play, too. Two go-cart tracks are separately designed for small children and teenagers. A snack trailer offers "county fair" treats such as funnel cakes, corn dogs, snow cones, and fresh lemonade. You can even rent a party room for birthdays and other celebrations.

Location: Texas 155 south of Tyler

Hours: Friday 5:00 - 11:00 p.m., Saturday 1:00 - 11:00 p.m., and Sunday 1:00 - 7:00 p.m.

HARROLD'S MODEL TRAIN MUSEUM

903-531-9404

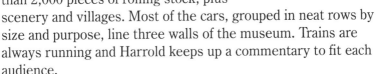

Harrold Little's train museum is a delight for railroad buffs. It has more than 2,000 pieces of rolling stock, plus scenery and villages. Most of the cars, grouped in neat rows by size and purpose, line three walls of the museum. Trains are always running and Harrold keeps up a commentary to fit each audience.

Location: Just off Loop 323 at 8103 North U.S. 271

Hours: Tuesday - Saturday 10:00 a.m. - 4:00 p.m.

Admission: $3.50/adults, $2/children and seniors

HUDNALL PLANETARIUM

903-510-2249

One of Texas' largest planetariums is on the campus of Tyler Junior College. The whole family will enjoy the multimedia presentations and monthly "star parties."

Location: 1200 S. Mahon

KIDS DEPOT

903-509-4386

Where kids can act like kids! They can climb and play until they're worn out at this children's recreation area. Designed for younger children.

Location: 5201 S. Broad

Hours: Monday - Thursday 9:30a.m. - 8:00 p.m., Friday and Saturday 9:00 a.m. - 9:00 p.m., Sunday 12:00 noon - 6:00 p.m.

Admission: $5.99/ ages 2-13

MUNICIPAL ROSE GARDEN AND MUSEUM

Roses! Roses! Roses! This 22-acre garden, the largest rose showcase in the U.S., features 38,000 rose bushes, representing nearly 500 varieties. Roses are at their floral peak May through November. Commercial growers around Tyler ship hundreds of thousands of bushes to nurseries throughout the U.S. and twenty-five foreign countries. The Rose Museum features educational exhibits of the rose-growing industry and displays former Rose Festival memorabilia.

Location: 420 South Rose Parkway

Hours: Gardens are open daily; Museum open Tuesday - Saturday 9:00 a.m. - 4:00 p.m.; Sun 1:30 - 4:00 p.m.; closed holidays

Tyler State Park

http://www.tpwd.state.tx.us/park/parks.htm

 This 994-acre scenic playground is in one of the most scenic forests of East Texas. Facilities include camping, picnicking, nature trails, screened shelters, snack bar, restrooms/showers, fishing, swimming, and boating.

Location: Ten miles north via FM 14, Park Road 16

Armadillo Willy's

Kids of all ages love this Texas-theme restaurant with lots of western memorabilia and cowboy decor.

215 WSW Loop 323

JW Finns

JW Finns is loads of fun, too. It's a Fifties-style diner, and they have kids' specials, "blue plate" specials, and a soda fountain.

2324 ESE Loop 323

Other:

Applebee's Skating Rink - regular and in-line skating - 903-581-1221

Family Fun Park - miniature golf, baseball and softball bating cages and Hoops USA basketball - 13731 Highway 110 South - 903-561-5537

UNCERTAIN

CADDO LAKE STATE PARK

http://www.tpwd.state.tx.us/park/parks.htm

One of the most popular recreation areas in East Texas, this 480-acre park borders the 32,000-acre Caddo Lake. The wildlife viewing and fishing are great! Facilities include campsites, shelters, and cabins, as well as swimming, fishing, boating, and hiking on the nature trails.

> Caddo Lake is the only naturally formed lake in Texas.

Location: West of town on FM 2198

Dozens of companies offer canoe and boat rental and tours. A few are:

- Caddo Canoe Rentals and Boat Tours - Scenic tours of Big Cypress Bayou and Caddo Lake. 903-679-3743

- Cypress Canoe Tours - Free canoeing lessons and detailed trail maps allow you to set your own pace through this primeval wonderland of majestic cypress trees covered with Spanish moss. 903-665-2911

- Caddo Lake Steamboat Company - Narrated tours of Caddo Lake aboard the *Graceful Ghost* steamboat, a replica of an 1890s paddle wheel riverboat. Daily 1½ hour tours March - November; closed December - mid-February. 888-325-5459 or 903-789-3978

> Lexie Palmore, owner of Caddo Lake Steamboat Company, is one of the few women licensed to pilot big barges on the Mississippi River.

175

Graceful Ghost steamboat (Caddo Lake Steamboat Company)
photo courtesy of Lexie Palmore

South Central

BASTROP

Chamber of Commerce
512-321-2419

BASTROP STATE PARK

http://www.tpwd.state.tx.us/park/parks.htm

This beautiful state park consists of 3,550 acres of quiet, rolling parklands shaded by the unusual "Lost Pines," an isolated area of stately pine trees far from the piney woods of East Texas. Facilities and activities include campsites, cabins, RV sites, picnicking, fishing, swimming, golf, and hiking.

Location: One mile east of Texas 21/71 intersection

CENTRAL TEXAS MUSEUM OF AUTOMOTIVE HISTORY

512-237-2635

See nearly eight decades of automotive history. Over 85 vintage cars are displayed, from Model Ts to a Duesenberg—some old, some rare, all beautiful.

Location: Twelve miles south on Texas 304

Hours: April - October: Wednesday - Saturday 9:00 a.m. - 5:00 p.m., Sunday 2:00 - 5:00 p.m.; November - March: Friday - Saturday 9:00 a.m. - 5:00 p.m., Sunday 2:00 - 5:00 p.m.

BRENHAM

see also: BURTON, INDEPENDENCE, WASHINGTON

Washington County Chamber of Commerce
314 S. Austin St.
888-BRENHAM or 409-836-3695
http://www.brenhamtx.org/

Brenham is a 152-year-old town that is the heart and soul of
Washington County. It's a charming little town with delightful
and diverse specialty shops and local artists. There are old-
fashioned soda fountains where cherry Cokes and sodas are still
made just like years ago. Downtown buildings reflect the town's
early history.

According to the July 1992 issue of *Texas Highways* magazine,
Washington County is the "best place in Texas to see wildflowers." Early March through late April is bluebonnet season, and
the visitor center distributes free "Bluebonnet Trails" maps that
follow the most scenic routes. In May and June vibrant colors
from Indian paintbrushes, Indian blankets, black-eyed Susans,
Mexican hats, thistles, pink evening primroses, and yellow core-
opsis cover nature's canvas—the rolling hills of Washington
County.

ANTIQUE CAROUSEL

409-836-7911

The kids of yesteryear will remember the alluring sound of the
merry-go-rounds and the thrill of riding hand-carved wooden
horses and chariots. Now another generation can see one of only
eight such antique carousels currently operating in Texas. If
you're lucky enough to visit during Maifest or other special
events, you can ride it for free. Built specifically for a traveling
carnival, this pre-1910 carousel has a mysterious history. Local
residents discovered the dilapidated horses, after years of

179

deterioration, in an open pasture. Now carefully restored, the vintage carousel resides in Fireman's Park inside a sixteen-sided stone building built by the WPA during the 1930s.

Location: Fireman's Park

Admission by group reservation only.

ANTIQUE ROSE EMPORIUM

409-836-5548

Do the children like roses or herbs or flowers? Try to entice them somehow, because this is a must for moms. The eight-acre retail display garden center is beautifully landscaped featuring romantic old garden roses, native plants, old-fashioned cottage garden perennials, herbs, and wildflowers.

Located on the grounds of an early homestead in historic Independence, the restored buildings include an 1855 stone kitchen original to the site, an 1940s log corn crib, an 1850s salt box house, and an early 1900s Victorian home.

Location: 9300 Lueckemeyer Rd.

Hours: Monday - Saturday 9:00 a.m. - 6:00 p.m., Sunday 11:00 a.m. - 5:30 p.m.; closed major holidays

Admission: FREE

BLUE BELL CREAMERIES

800-327-8135
http://www.bluebell.com/

You can have a scoop of your favorite ice cream at the end of the tour! Kids of all ages may take a 45-minute tour to see how Blue Bell ice cream is made. Suggest an idea for a new flavor— they're always on the lookout for new ones. Blue Bell originated Cookies 'n Cream, their second best-seller behind Homemade

Vanilla. This revered Texas treat began in 1911 when the Brenham Creamery Company decided to supplement its butter production by making a few gallons of ice cream. And, as they say, the rest is history. The name was changed to Blue Bell Creameries (for the wildflowers that cover the hillsides in spring), but otherwise little has changed. Although thousands of gallons are now made hourly, quality ingredients still make up the ice cream considered the absolute best by most Texans. The Blue Bell Country Store specializes in logo items and country gifts.

Location: FM 577 about two miles north of U.S. 290

Hours: Tours on weekdays only, on a first-come, first-served basis. Groups of 15 or more are required to make reservations. During spring break, reservations are required for all visitors.

Admission: $2/adults, $1.50/seniors (55+) and children 6-14, FREE for children under 6 (includes a serving of Blue Bell ice cream)

Blue Bell Creameries
Photo courtesy of Scott Hill, Brenham Portrait Gallery

Brenham Heritage Museum

409-830-8445

Built in 1915 to house the U.S. post office, this distinctive Classical Revival style building became the home of the Brenham Heritage Museum in 1991. Here, children can see the Silsby Steam Fire Engine, purchased by the City of Brenham in 1879 for $3,000, a fortune in those days. Permanent exhibits depict the diverse history of Washington County, and special exhibits are presented throughout the year. Wheelchair accessible.

Location: 105 S. Market St.

Hours: Wednesday 1 p.m. - 4 p.m., Thursday - Saturday 10 a.m. - 4 p.m.

Admission: FREE, donations appreciated

Burton Farmers Gin—see: Burton

Citizens Pharmacy and Glissmann Drug Store

Treat your kids to a part of your past. Buy them an old-fashioned cherry Coke or soda, made just as they were years ago, at either of these soda fountains. Citizens is a working drugstore and has a grill where they make good hamburgers, too. Glissmann's, in an 1860 building, has a soda fountain, pharmaceutical museum, and a gift shop with such specialties as gourmet coffees, teas, and chocolates. Both are wheelchair accessible.

Location: Citizens: 201 E. Main, Glissmann: 106 W. Main

La Bahia Road

This scenic route follows the historic La Bahia Road through rolling meadows, fields of spring wildflowers, and past picturesque horse ranches and country estates. See if you can tell which of the dairy cattle are the "contented cows" of Blue Bell Creameries fame. This is a delightful drive that will lead you to Independence where Texas history abounds. Visit the Independence Baptist Church where Sam Houston was converted and baptized and the graves of his wife and mother-in-law in the small cemetery across from the church. If you're a Baylor University graduate (or not), it's interesting to see where it was organized in 1845 as two separate schools—one for women and one for men, located at opposite sides of the town. Explain that to your modern-day child.

Location: Hwy. 390

LAKE SOMERVILLE STATE PARK

http://www.tpwd.state.tx.us/park/parks.htm

Swim, boat, or fish on the 11,640-acre Lake Somerville. Two major recreation areas offer camping areas, horseback riding, hiking and biking trails, and some wheelchair accessible trails. Access the Birch Creek Unit recreation area from the north and the Nails Creek recreation area from the south.

Location: Fifteen miles northwest of Brenham

THE MONASTERY OF ST. CLARE MINIATURE HORSE RANCH

409-836-9652

Yes, you may pet the horses. Some of these miniature thoroughbred horses are only 30 inches in height. And tiny foals are born every year between February and April. The Monastery is home to a group of Franciscan Poor Clare nuns who support themselves by raising the miniature horses and by selling handmade ceramic wares, handpainted gifts, and horse-related items in the "Art Barn" gift shop. Also on the grounds are a stable, picnic area, and lovely chapel where guests are welcome. A visit to this convent will be a memorable experience for all.

Location: 9300 Texas 105, nine miles east of Brenham

Hours: Daily 2:00 - 4:00 p.m., except during Holy Week and
Christmas Day; groups may schedule a 45-minute guided tour
for $3/adult, $1/children

Admission: FREE, donations appreciated

STAR OF THE REPUBLIC MUSEUM—see: WASHINGTON

WASHINGTON-ON-THE-BRAZOS STATE PARK—see: WASHINGTON

SPECIAL EVENTS

TEXAS INDEPENDENCE DAY

This giant birthday party is celebrated on the
Saturday or Sunday nearest March 2 at
Washington-on-the-Brazos State Historical Park.

MAIFEST

One of the oldest German festivals in Texas, this has been an
annual event in Brenham since 1884, except for a few years during both world wars. Merrymakers enjoy continuous polka and
waltz music, wurst and kraut, arts and crafts, a parade with
floats and bands, and pageants.

BRYAN-COLLEGE STATION

Convention and Visitors Bureau
715 University Dr. East
800-777-8292 or 409-260-9898

GEORGE BUSH PRESIDENTIAL LIBRARY AND MUSEUM

http://www.csdl.tamu.edu/bushlib/

This 69,000-square-foot library and museum is dedicated to the preservation and research of official records, personal papers, and memorabilia from the life and career of George Bush. One section is devoted to Barbara Bush's activities, from her promotion of literacy to her book about their dog Millie.

Location: 1000 George Bush Drive West on Texas A&M University campus

Hours: Monday - Saturday 9:30 a.m. - 5:00 p.m., Sunday noon - 5:00 p.m.; closed New Year's Day, Thanksgiving, and Christmas

Admission: $3/adults; $2.50/seniors, A&M and Blinn faculty, and students with ID; free for children 16 and under

TEXAS A&M UNIVERSITY

http://www.tamu.edu/

Famed for its military Cadet Corps and ROTC, this university has outstanding research and experimental facilities in agriculture, animal pathology, salt and freshwater fisheries, engineering, and nuclear technology. Several interesting exhibits and programs are open to the public.

Location: Information Center in Rudder Tower

Hours: Monday - Friday 9:00 a.m. - 5:00 p.m.

BURTON

http://www.brenhamtx.org/

BURTON FARMERS GIN

409-289-3378

Cotton once reigned supreme in the Brazos Valley. A rare working cotton gin from this era exists in the tiny town of Burton. Operation Restoration, Inc. is restoring the 1914 gin and other historical properties to become part of a national museum complex for cotton ginning and cotton fiber production.

Location: About 12 miles west of Brenham on U.S. 290

Admission: $2

COLUMBUS

Visitor Information Center
Stafford Opera House
409-732-8385
http://users.intertex.net/ccvb/

COLUMBUS OPRY

409-732-6510

Have a rollicking good time and stomp your feet as you enjoy live entertainment every Saturday night in the historic Oaks Theater, two blocks west of the town square. The performances could be country-western "Grand Ol' Opry" style, jubilant gospel singing, or oom-pah polka music.

Location: 715 Walnut St.

Hours: Saturday performance: 7:30 - 10:00 p.m. (doors open at 6:30)

Admission: $6/adults, $3/children 6-12, children under 6 free

Santa Claus Museum

This extraordinary collection of over 2,000 Santa Clauses is dedicated to the memory of Mary Elizabeth Hopkins. She was only six months old in 1913 when her parents gave her a Santa for Christmas. It began her lifetime collection that ended with a Santa purchased in 1990 a short time before her death. There's a Santa of every size, shape, artistic style, and material imaginable.

Location: 604 Washington

Gonzales

Chamber of Commerce
In the old 1887 jail house
888-672-1095

Gonzales Memorial Museum

This small-town museum is a nice tribute to those who fought the first battle of the Texas Revolution. On display is a replica of the cannon that precipitated that first battle when Texans challenged Mexican troops to "Come and take it."

Location: E. St. Lawrence St.

Hours: Tuesday - Saturday 10:00 a.m. - 5:00 p.m., Sunday 1:00 - 5:00 p.m.

PALMETTO STATE PARK
830/672-3266
http://www.tpwd.state.tx.us/park/parks.htm

Along the San Marcos River, this park was named for the tropical dwarf palmetto found there. The handsome stone buildings in the park were constructed by the CCC during the 1930s. This is an unusual botanical area that resembles the tropics more than Central Texas.

Facilities include campsites, a group picnic shelter with kitchen, restrooms with showers, playgrounds, a trailer dump station, picnic tables, and interpretive and hiking trails. Rental pedal boats and horseshoes are available at the Texas State Park Store.

Location: Northwest of Gonzales via U.S. 183, FM 1586, and Park Road 11

LA GRANGE

Chamber of Commerce
800-LA GRANGE or 409-968-5756

THE JERSEY BARNYARD
409-249-3406
http://www.texasjersey.com/barn/

What a fun place to visit. Take a tractor-drawn hayride to the dairy. See cow-milking demonstrations (you can try it if you want) and learn all about the animals. Feed and pet the goats, donkey, bunnies, ducks, calves, and more. Visit Belle, the famous "singing cow" from Blue Bell Creameries. Then visit the Jersey General Store for gifts, crafts, souvenirs, or a hand-dipped cone of Blue Bell ice cream.

Location: 3117 Hwy. 159

Hours: Monday - Friday 10:00 a.m. - 6:00 p.m., Saturday 9:00 a.m. - 6:00 p.m., Sunday 1:00 - 6:00 p.m. Tours unavailable on Wednesdays

Admission: $4/adults and children ages 2 and over, free for children under 2

PLANTERSVILLE

SPECIAL EVENT

TEXAS RENAISSANCE FESTIVAL
800-458-3435
www.texrenfest.com

Discover medieval Europe—men wearing plumed hats and embroidered waistcoats, women in elegant long gowns, harlequin jesters, minstrels, armored knights, magicians, and raffish gypsies. Watch jousting, juggling, and dancing. Taste delicious foods from the king's banquet hall: giant turkey legs, sweet mead wine, roasted corn, apple dumplings, and more. Plan to spend the day. Stroller and wheelchair rentals are available.

Location: Six miles south of Plantersville on FM 1774

Hours: Seven fall weekends in October and November: 9:00 a.m. - dusk

ROUND TOP

http://www.roundtop.com/

Round Top claims to be the smallest incorporated city in Texas with a population of 81. Over 100,000 people invade the tiny town each April and October for one of the largest antique shows in the U.S.

INTERNATIONAL FESTIVAL INSTITUTE

409-249-3129
http://www.fais.net/~festinst/

Founded by acclaimed pianist James Dick, this is a world-renowned facility set on 80 scenic acres of central Texas. The landscaped campus features gardens, historic buildings, and the concert hall which seats 1,200. Various concerts are performed throughout the year, and in summer students in residence from throughout the world join the distinguished performers and teachers.

Location: Texas 237

WINEDALE HISTORICAL CENTER

409-278-3530

Numerous educational activities and special events go on during the year at this restored nineteenth-entury farmstead. See plantation homes, log cabins, a fireplace kitchen, smokehouse, and barns. It's the Center for the Study of Ethnic Cultures of Central Texas, operated by the University of Texas. The property also serves as a site for seminars, arts and crafts festivals, and performances of plays and folk music.

Location: Four miles east via FM 1457 and FM 2714

Hours: Saturday 9:00 a.m. - 5:00 p.m., Sunday noon - 5:00 p.m.

KLUMP'S

409-249-5696

Located in the old tinsmith shop, this is a dandy place for plate lunches, sandwiches, and great burgers. Specials include catfish on Fridays and fried chicken on Sundays.

ROYER'S ROUND TOP CAFE

409-249-3611

It's the classic small town cafe. On the town square. It serves great food for lunch and dinner and is widely acclaimed for homemade pies. Folks come from miles around for the good cookin' and down-home ambience.

Hours: Wednesday - Sunday

SAN FELIPE

STEPHEN F. AUSTIN STATE PARK

http://www.tpwd.state.tx.us/park/parks.htm

This 664-acre park is in two sections, historical and recreational. The historical section is near an old ferry crossing of the Brazos River. The restored J.J. Josey Store, built in 1847, is now a museum displaying merchandise of the pioneer era.

The recreational portion of the park offers picnic areas, camping and trailer sites, a recreational hall, nature trail, and a golf course.

Location: Just north of San Felipe on Park Road 38

Hours: Museum open weekends only

SEALY

RIVER BRIDGE SAFARI AND SUPERPARK

281-375-6911

There's something for everyone here. Choose from or enjoy all—a drive-through exotic animal safari, go-carts, miniature golf, tree houses, horseback riding, pony rides, hayrides, train rides, swimming, and picnicking.

Location: Take the Peach Ridge Rd. exit. Stay on feeder road to the Brazos River, take Siedel Rd. to the park entrance.

Hours: Wednesday - Sunday 10:00 a.m. - 6:00 p.m.

SEGUIN

Convention & Visitors Bureau
427 N. Austin
800-580-7322 or 830-379-6382
http://www.seguin.net/corp/segcvb

MAX STARCKE PARK

This is one of the finest municipal parks for a city of this size in the nation. A beautiful drive winds along the Guadalupe River beneath towering oak and pecan trees. Facilities include a golf course, swimming pool, playground, and picnic areas. A gigantic wave pool is open in the summer months.

Location: Off Texas 123 at the Guadalupe River

SMITHVILLE

RAILROAD HISTORICAL PARK AND MUSEUM

512-237-2313

As you would expect, this museum depicts the history of the railroad in Smithville and its importance to the community. Exhibits include Union Pacific and Missouri-Kansas-Texas (Katy) cabooses, photographs, and railroad memorabilia. The Katy depot was built from materials salvaged from a former station built in the 1890s. The gazebo in the adjacent park is topped by a cupola from the 1896 city hall.

Location: 102 W. First St.

Hours: Monday - Friday 9:00 a.m. - 5:00 p.m.

WASHINGTON

http://www.brenhamtx.org/

STAR OF THE REPUBLIC MUSEUM

409-878-2461

Located within the Washington-on-the-Brazos State Historical Park, this outstanding museum depicts the colorful saga of Texas and its heritage. Through audiovisual presentations and exhibits, learn about the heroes and legends and cattlemen and farmers who settled and fought for Texas. The "Childhood in Texas" exhibit features antique dolls and toys. All facilities in the museum and the park are wheelchair accessible.

Hours: Daily 10:00 a.m. - 5:00 p.m.

Admission: FREE

WASHINGTON-ON-THE-BRAZOS STATE HISTORICAL PARK

409-878-2214
http://www.tpwd.state.tx.us/park/parks.htm

Experience the nineteenth-century lifestyle through living history re-enactments with demonstrations of such crafts as spinning and weaving, blacksmithing, and candle-making. Join thousands of merrymakers the Saturday or Sunday nearest March 2 for the rollicking birthday party celebrating Texas Independence Day. Revered as the "Birthplace of Texas," the site of the signing of the Texas Declaration of Independence is fascinating for all and a must for Texans.

After an extensive $6 million renovation in 1997, the park offers a visitor center with interactive exhibits and a gift shop, a conference center featuring a full-service restaurant, and an education center. Independence Hall and the Washington Townsite tell the story of the beginning of Texas with exhibits and living history programs.

Barrington, the home of Anson Jones, the last president of the Republic of Texas, is a living history farm representing a working farm of the 1850s with livestock and a costumed staff. Children's Fishing Derby, Pioneer Day Camp, and Junior Ranger Camp are among the numerous special events for children.

Location: Just off Texas 105 between Brenham and Navasota

Hours: Park headquarters open daily 9:00 a.m. - 5:00 p.m.; grounds open daily 8:00 a.m. - sundown

Admission: FREE

YOAKUM

Visit the Leather Capital Store, a western outlet store, set amid displays of the Old West. It features a wide selection of leather goods from all the leather factories in Yoakum.

HERITAGE MUSEUM

Much of the heritage of Yoakum is centered around leather. The Leather Room features the history of the leather industry from the old Chisholm Trail cattle drives to the first tannery with displays of vintage leather products from the turn of the century. Exhibits also show the creative workmanship in leather goods today.

Location: 312 Simpson St.

Hours: Tuesday, Thursday, Friday 1:00 - 5:00 p.m., Sunday 2:00 - 5:00 p.m.

South East

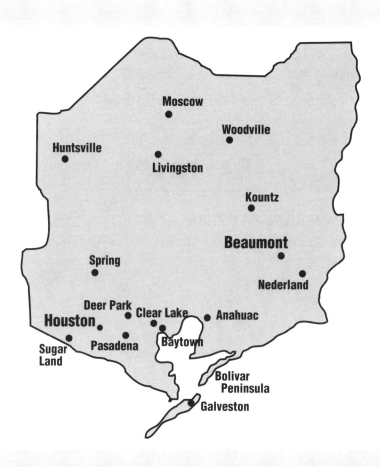

ANAHUAC

ANAHUAC NATIONAL WILDLIFE REFUGE

409-267-3337

http://sturgeon.irm1.r2.fws.gov/u2/refuges/texas/anahuac.html

Along the Gulf of Mexico, this 24,356-acre marshland on East Bay is managed primarily for wintering and migrating waterfowl. A bird checklist has 253 species listed. Refuge activities include wildlife observation, birding, photography, fishing, and crabbing. Limited overnight camping.

Location: About 18 miles southeast of Anahuac

BAYTOWN

HOUSTON RACEWAY PARK

This 440-acre drag racing complex has races every Wednesday and Saturday night.

Location: 2525 FM 5656 South

LYNCHBURG FERRY

In operation since 1822, the Lynchburg ferry shuttles travelers across the mouth of the San Jacinto River.

Location: West of town

BEAUMONT

Beaumont Convention & Visitors Bureau
801 Main, Suite 100
800-392-4401 or 409-880-3749
http://www.tourtexas.com/beaumont/

BABE DIDRIKSON ZAHARIAS MUSEUM AND VISITOR CENTER

800-392-4401 or 409-833-4622

Learn about this Texas heroine, Beaumont's Mildred "Babe" Didrikson Zaharias (1914-1956). One of the most versatile athletes in history, she was three-time basketball All-American, won three Olympic gold medals, and was a world-class pioneering woman golfer. Her trophies and memorabilia are displayed here. A visitor center provides information, maps, and brochures for the area.

Location: 1750 I-10 and Martin Luther King Parkway, exit 854

Hours: Daily 9:00 a.m. - 5:00 p.m.

Admission: FREE

BEAUMONT POLICE MUSEUM

409-880-3825

Another unusual museum, this one features a vast collection of police memorabilia dating to the turn of the century.

Location: 255 College

Hours: Monday - Friday 8:00 a.m. - 5:00 p.m.

CLIFTON STEAMBOAT MUSEUM

409-842-3162

"Heroes . . . Past, Present and Future" is the museum's theme. This 24,000 square-foot facility honors military and civilian heroes with a huge variety of exhibits from the Battle of San Jacinto and the Republic of Texas and its statehood to the steamboat era to the world wars. There's also a gift shop, a frame shop/art gallery, restaurant, and See-Max Theater.

Location: 8727 Fannett Rd.

Hours: Monday - Saturday 9:00 a.m. - 5:00 p.m., Sunday noon - 5:00 p.m.

FIRE MUSEUM OF TEXAS

409-880-3927

Another interesting museum, this 1927 former fire station displays vintage fire engines, antique fire bells, leather buckets, photographs, and other memorabilia. Upstairs, a "Fire Safety Activity Center" teaches fire prevention and features a safety house, toy collection, and a puppet theater.

Location: In the Old Central Fire Station at 400 Walnut

Fire Museum of Texas
Photo courtesy of Beaumont
Convention & Visitors Bureau

Hours: Monday - Friday 8:00 a.m. - 4:30 p.m.

Admission: FREE

Port of Beaumont

409-832-1546

See a deepwater port in action! This is a favorite tour for children and adults.

Location: 1255 Main St.

Hours: Daily 8:00 a.m. - noon and 1:00 - 5:00 p.m.

Admission: FREE

Port of Beaumont
Photo courtesy of
Beaumont Convention
& Visitors Bureau

SPINDLETOP/GLADYS CITY BOOMTOWN

409-835-0823

Every Texan knows the story of Spindletop. The world's first oil boomtown is re-created here with typical clapboard buildings of the era, including a post office, saloon, livery stable, blacksmith shop, surveyor's office, and wooden oil derricks.

Location: University Dr. at U.S. 69 South

Hours: Tuesday - Sunday 1:00 - 5:00 p.m.

TYRRELL PARK

BEAUMONT BOTANICAL GARDENS AND WARREN LOOSE CONSERVATORY

This lovely park has an 18-hole golf course, playground, bridle and hiking trails, and a cattail marsh amid 500 acres of woodlands.

Within the park, Beaumont's Botanical Gardens are magnificent, some of the best display gardens in the state. Wander and enjoy the Japanese Garden, Antique Rose Garden, Formal Rose Garden, Azalea Walk (incredible in springtime), herb and wildflower gardens, ponds, and pools. The paved walkway connecting the gardens is easily wheelchair accessible.

The Warren Loose Conservatory opened in late 1997 displaying thousands of tropical plants in an enchanted setting. At one end, an animated dinosaur watches over the area.

Location: Tyrrell Park Rd. off Fannett (Texas 124)

Hours: Botanical Gardens: Daily 7:30 a.m. - dusk

Conservatory: Saturday 10:00 a.m. - 5:00 p.m., Sunday 1:00 - 5:00 p.m.

Admission: Botanical Gardens: FREE

Conservatory: $3/adults, $2/seniors, $1/children ages 6-12

BOLIVAR PENINSULA

(Crystal Beach)
Chamber of Commerce
800-FUN-SUN3
409-684-5940
www.bolivar.com

Miles of sandy beaches offer innumerable recreational activities.
Ride the ferry between Port Bolivar and Galveston and see the
old Bolivar Lighthouse, still standing near Texas 87.

CLEAR LAKE AREA

(Clear Lake Shores, El Lago, Kemah, League City,
Nassau Bay, Seabrook, Taylor Lake Village, Webster,
and NASA/Johnson Space Center)
Clear Lake Area CVB
1201 NASA Road 1
800-844-5253 or 281-488-7676

SPACE CENTER HOUSTON

800-972-0369 or 281-244-2105
http://www.spacecenter.org

Touch a moon rock. Practice landing a space shuttle with a computer simulator. See how astronauts eat, sleep, and work while
living in space. This state-of-the-art complex serves as the visitor center for NASA/Johnson Space Center. The Center provides
an adventure into the past, present, and future of NASA's

manned space flight program with interactive exhibits, IMAX films, and behind-the-scenes tram tours of Johnson Space Center, home of America's astronauts. See a Mercury capsule, Gemini spacecraft, and Apollo 17 command module displayed in simulated natural settings.

"Kids Space Place" is a hands-on play arena that lets kids experience space through interactive activities. Ride in the Lunar Rover and walk on the moon to experience weightlessness.

Location: NASA Road 1, three miles east of I-45

Hours: Monday - Friday 10:00 a.m. - 5:00 p.m. (10:00 a.m. - 7:00 p.m. in the summer), Saturday, Sunday, and holidays 10:00 a.m. - 7:00 p.m.

Admission: $12.95/adults, $8.95/ages 4-11

TEXAS ICE STADIUM

281-286-7979

What an ice-skating rink! This premier facility has 50,000 square feet of ice, locker rooms, party/event rooms, pro shop, childcare area, and a restaurant. Public skating, hockey, and figure skating events are hosted. Call for rates and hours.

Location: I-45 South, exit Clear Lake City Blvd.

DEER PARK

SAN JACINTO BATTLEGROUND STATE HISTORIC PARK

http://www.tpwd.state.tx.us/park/parks.htm

Stand on the site where Texas won its independence from Mexico on April 21, 1836! The Battle of San Jacinto took place right here. The majestic San Jacinto monument soars 570 feet above the flat coastal plain, marking the battlefield. At the base of the monument is the San Jacinto Museum of Texas History. "Texas Forever! The Battle of San Jacinto" is a 35-minute history lesson from the days of Spanish rule in Mexico to the expansion of the American West in 1848. This spectacular multi-image presentation uses forty-two projectors.

The battleship *Texas* is moored in a permanent slip at the San Jacinto battleground. One of the few monuments of its kind in the world, the battleship was presented to the state of Texas by the U.S. Navy. It served in both World Wars, and in the 1944 D-Day invasion it was commanded by General Dwight D. Eisenhower, a native of Denison, Texas.

Location: East of downtown Houston, about 22 miles via Texas 225 and Texas 134

Hours: Museum: Daily 9:00 a.m. - 6:00 p.m.

Elevator and observation deck: Daily 10:00 a.m. - 5:30 p.m.

Battleship: Wednesday - Sunday 10:00 a.m. - 5:00 p.m.

Admission: For elevator ride and for "Texas Forever!" show

GALVESTON

Visitor Information Centers
In Moody Civic Center: Seawall Blvd. at 21st St.
In Strand Historic District: 2016 Strand
http://www.galvestontourism.com/

Galveston Island offers thirty-two miles of beach and tons of Texas history. City parks, picnic areas, and recreation centers offer playground equipment, athletic fields, tennis courts, and

golf courses. Several companies offer deep-sea fishing excursions.

DAVID TAYLOR CLASSIC CAR MUSEUM

A tribute to American automobiles, this collection is divided into three categories: antiques, classics, and muscle cars, and is exhibited in three restored buildings that look like car dealerships of the 1930s.

Location: 1918 Mechanic St.

Hours: Daily 10:00 a.m. - 5:00 p.m.

GALVESTON COUNTY HISTORICAL MUSEUM

The building that houses this museum is a former private bank building, circa 1919, with a splendid interior. The museum itself showcases one of Texas' most historic cities.

Location: 2219 Market St.

Hours: Monday - Saturday 10:00 a.m. - 4:00 p.m., Sunday 12:00 noon - 4:00 p.m.; extended hours Memorial Day - Labor Day

GALVESTON ISLAND STATE PARK

http://www.tpwd.state.tx.us/park/parks.htm

Spanning Galveston Island from the Gulf of Mexico to the West Bay, this 1,935-acre park includes salt marshes rich in bird life. Facilities include campsites, screened shelters, and restrooms/showers. Fish, swim, picnic, and stroll nature trails.

THE GREAT STORM

This award winning, multi-image presentation uses historic photographs and special effects to re-create the aftermath of the

1900 hurricane that devastated Galveston. The 27-minute program shows on the hour.

Location: Pier 21 at the north end of 21st St.

Hours: Sunday - Thursday 11:00 a.m. - 6:00 p.m., Friday and Saturday 11:00 a.m. - 8:00 p.m.

LONE STAR FLIGHT MUSEUM

Two dozen vintage aircraft, including a meticulously restored B-17 Flying Fortress, recall the golden age of aviation. The Conoco Hall of Power features old engines, photos, air combat memorabilia, and wartime vehicles.

Location: Scholes Field Municipal Airport, 2002 Terminal Drive

Hours: Daily 10:00 a.m. - 5:00 p.m.; closed major holidays

MOODY GARDENS

800-582-4673
http://www.moodygardens.com/core/attractions/index.html

Children and adults can spend the entire day at this incredible 156-acre complex. Within the complex are a visitor center, The Gardens restaurant overlooking the Gulf, and a nightly presentation of "dancing waters."

- Rainforest Pyramid: Experience the exotic rain forest—butterflies flitting among waterfalls, cliffs, caverns, and an ever-changing array of exotic tropical plants. Soaring ten stories, this glass pyramid represents rain forests of the world. Its clear, blue pools are filled with tropical fish, and quiet ponds are filled with exotic wading birds. A "Bat Cave" turns night into day, so you can watch fruit bats behind large glass panels.

- IMAX 3D Theater Complex: The moment you slip on your 3D glasses, you become part of the action. Explore the

depths of the world's oceans or the far reaches of outer
space. Images seem to leap from the six-story screen. Call
for films and schedule.

- Discovery Pyramid: The wonders of space come into amazing focus in this pyramid, the second in the trio. NASA's
  Johnson Space Center and Moody Gardens teamed up to
  develop the unique exhibits. The IMAX Ridefilm Theater
  offers thrilling motion-based films. Strap on your seatbelt and
  hold on for a ride across the cosmos at warp speed! The
  180-degree wraparound screen and realistic IMAX sound
  brings the action alive.

- Palm Beach: Bring the kids and enjoy a day at Texas' only
  white sand beach. Okay, so the sand was barged in from Flor-
  ida. Relax amid clear freshwater swimming lagoons,
  waterfalls, lush landscaping, and soothing waters of Texas-
  sized spas. Let the kids play volleyball on the white sand,
  ride the paddleboats, or play on the Octopus Slippery Slides.
  Inside the 30-foot Yellow Submarine, the kids can operate the
  periscope, water gun, and control panels. It features padded
  foam surfaces and is especially adapted for wheelchair
  access. Open daily mid-May - Labor Day. 409-744-PALM

- Aquarium Pyramid: A spectacular two-million-gallon tribute
  to the fascinating oceans of the world will be the third of the
  glass pyramid trio and is scheduled to open in 1999.

Hours: Most of the attractions are open Memorial Day - Labor
Day: daily 10:00 a.m. - 9:00 p.m. and Labor Day - Memorial Day:
Sunday - Thursday 10:00 a.m. - 6:00 p.m., Friday and Saturday
10:00 a.m. - 9:00 p.m. Call for details.

OCEAN STAR OFFSHORE DRILLING RIG AND MUSEUM
409-766-7827

This state-of-the-art facility gives visitors a better understand-
ing of how oil and gas are produced offshore. Tour the

refurbished jackup and learn about drilling procedures and production, marine transportation, and environmental protection. It's a museum, educational facility, and drilling rig all in one.

Location: Adjacent to Pier 19 on Harborside Dr.

Hours: Daily 10:00 a.m. - 5:00 p.m. (10:00 a.m. - 4:00 p.m. in winter)

RAILROAD MUSEUM

Don't miss one of the best railroad museums in the country. Thirty-five vintage railroad cars and steam engines sit on once-active tracks at the historic Santa Fe depot, restored to its 1932 Art Deco-era splendor. An HO-gauge working model of the Port of Galveston is complete with tracks, ships, and port activities. The People's Gallery features dozens of life-sized figures  re-creating a busy depot scene of the 1930s. Don't jump when some of the figures "speak" to you. Six multimedia theaters present the history of Galveston's shipping, railroading, and commerce.

Location: Center for Transportation and Commerce on Rosenberg St.

Hours: Daily 10:00 a.m. - 5:00 p.m.

SEA CAMP

409-740-4525
http://www.tamug.tamu.edu/~seacamp/

Offered by Texas A&M University at Galveston, this is a five-day adventure for ten- to eighteen-year-olds. Exploring the wonders of the marine environment, participants have access to research vessels, oceanographic equipment, laboratory facilities,

and a professional staff enabling them to learn about the ocean through firsthand experiences.

SEAWOLF PARK

Hang out at this park to get a close look at ocean-going vessels entering and departing the port and yacht basin. It's said the fishing is good from the commercially operated pier. There's also a three-level pavilion with a snack bar, picnic facilities, and children's playground. Another attraction is a naval exhibit where you can tour the WW II submarine USS *Cavalla*, the destroyer escort USS *Stewart*, a Navy jet, and other military vehicles.

Location: On Pelican Island

TEXAS SEAPORT MUSEUM

409-763-1877
http://www.phoenix.net/~tsm/default.html
http://www.texashighways.com/elissa1.html

Don't miss this one! This is the home of the *Elissa*, a 400-ton, 202-foot square-rigged iron barque, the third oldest ship afloat, built in Scotland in 1877. Today, the *Elissa* is a museum, a tribute to nineteenth-century maritime technology. It includes two wide-screen theater presentations: one about the restoration of the *Elissa*, the other on legends and lore of the sea. This magnificent ship was opened to the public in 1982 after eight years of restoration. Volunteers restored it and continue its upkeep every weekend; they'll probably be around to demonstrate setting sails and handling lines.

Location: Pier 21 at the north end of Kempner (22nd) St.

Hours: Daily from 10:00 a.m. - 5:00 p.m. with extended hours in summer

Admission: $5/ adults, $4/students, free for kids under age seven

TOURS:

- *The Colonel*, excursion boat - Ride a Victorian-style double-decker paddle wheel boat, reminiscent of the great steamboat era, on sightseeing cruises of Galveston Bay. *The Colonel* departs from Moody Gardens at One Hope Blvd. 409-740-7797

- Ferry rides - Ride a diesel ferry between Galveston and Port Bolivar. They run every 20 minutes as part of the Texas highway system, operated toll-free by Texas D.O.T.

- Galveston harbor tours - The M/V *Seagull* entertains passengers on a 45-minute narrated boat tour of the Port of Galveston. Departs from Pier 22 at the north end of 22nd Street. 409-765-1700

- Trolley cars - Old-fashioned trolley cars connect the beach at the seawall to the historic Strand/Bay area. The trolley provides a unique mode of transportation with beautiful historic homes and other points of interest along the route. 409-763-4311

HOUSTON

800-4-HOUSTON
http://www.houston-guide.com/

Due to the immense variety and number of kid-friendly attractions in major metropolitan areas, only a few are listed, and you're encouraged to visit the local visitor information center for more detailed information.

ADVENTURE BAY

281-498-7946
http://www.adventurebay.com/

What kid wouldn't enjoy splashing about twelve acres of water fun! Ride Houston's only "Master Blaster," a water coaster that defies gravity and sends its riders uphill! Explore Pirates Cove with its huge interactive pirate ship. For the adventurous, there are plenty of thrills. For the less adventurous, try the lazy river or the wave pool. There's also a full service food and beverage court.

Location: 13602 Beechnut at Eldridge in southwest Houston

Hours: Memorial Day - Labor Day

CELEBRATION STATION

281-872-7778 and 713-981-7888

Amusements and games include go-carts, bumper boats, a challenging miniature golf course, and food court.

Location: 180 W Rankin Rd. and 6767 Southwest Fwy.

Hours: Vary with the season

CHILDREN'S MUSEUM

http://www.cmhouston.org/

Family Fun magazine readers voted this one of the top ten children's museums in the nation. It offers a tremendous variety of hands-on exhibits for children up to age fourteen in the areas of science, history, culture, and the arts. There's a wonderful outdoor discovery garden and greenhouse.

Location: 1500 Binz in the Museum District

Hours: Tuesday - Saturday 9:00 a.m. - 5:00 p.m., Sunday 12:00 noon - 5:00 p.m.

HOUSTON ZOO

713-284-1300
http://www.houstonzoo.org/

You can easily spend most of a day at the Houston Zoo, renowned as one of the most unusual zoos in the U.S. It features a tropical bird house representative of an Asian jungle with over two hundred exotic birds flying freely through a rain forest. Other areas of interest include a hippo-dome, a large cat facility with rare white tigers, a large collection of reptiles, and vampire bats. The Wortham World of Primates is a large rain forest and natural habitat for primates.

Location: Hermann Park

Hours: Tuesday - Sunday 10:00 a.m. - 6:00 p.m.

MALIBU GRAND PRIX FAMILY ENTERTAINMENT CENTER

713-683-8255

This chain amusement park features its landmark castle and indoor/outdoor race track, bumper boats, miniature golf, batting cages, and to-scale Indy 500 race cars. The castle interior offers skill-testing games.

Location: 1111 W. Loop North

MOUNTASIA FAMILY FUN CENTER

281-894-9791

Another chain amusement park with fun in a fantasy format. Activities include miniature golf, bumper boats, go-carts, batting cages, and indoor game rooms.

Location: 11175 Katy Fwy. and 17190 Tomball Pkwy.

ORANGE SHOW

713-926-6368

Truly a "you've-got-to-see-it-to-believe-it" attraction. Virtually impossible to describe, this is the masterpiece of a Houston eccentric assembled over twenty-six years. An indoor-outdoor labyrinth of passages, stairs, and platforms amid colorful whirligigs, gewgaws, folk art, and junk. Bizarre!

Location: 2402 Munger Street

Hours: Weekends and holidays

Admission: $1/adults, free for children

THE REEF

713-991-3483
281-597-2970—24-hour information line
http://www.atthereef.com/

Talk about fun! You can swim in the beautiful 20-acre spring-fed lake, play volleyball on two courts, try your skill at the 500 meter swim course, play on the family beach or the children's activity beach, or scuba dive. Rent a boat, kayak, or tube for more water fun or just lounge around and watch the abundant wildlife and enjoy the picnic areas.

Location: 4800 Schurmier Rd. on the south side of Houston

Hours: May - September: Monday - Friday 11:00 a.m. - 8:00 p.m., Saturday and Sunday 7:00 a.m. - 8:00 p.m.; September - May: Saturday and Sunday 9:00 a.m. - 4:00 p.m.

Admission: $7/adult, $5.50/teens, seniors, students, $3/children

SAN JACINTO BATTLEGROUND STATE HISTORIC PARK—see: DEER PARK

SIX FLAGS ASTROWORLD/WATERWORLD

713-799-1234
http://www.sixflags.com/parks/

Taz's Texas Tornado is one of the newest rides opened in 1998 to celebrate the park's thirtieth anniversary. This 112-foot roller coaster has four huge loops and 3,280 feet of track. Six Flags AstroWorld features more rides than any park in Texas, including eleven roller coasters, the most in Texas and the third highest number in the world. Six Flags WaterWorld has a wide variety of water slides and swings, a 30,000-square-foot wave pool, and a children's water play area.

Location: Loop 610 at Kirby Dr.

Hours: Daily in summer, weekends spring and fall

AstroWorld Admission: $32.95/adult, $21.95 seniors and children under 48 inches, 3 and under free, discounts for disabled persons and for two-day passes

WaterWorld Admission: $16.95 adult, $13.96 seniors and children under 48 inches, 3 and under free, discounts for disabled persons

SPACE CENTER HOUSTON—see: CLEAR LAKE AREA

SPLASH TOWN WATERPARK—see: SPRING

HUNTSVILLE

Huntsville-Walker County Chamber of Commerce
800-289-0389
http://chamber.huntsville.tx.us/tourism.html

HUNTSVILLE STATE PARK

http://www.tpwd.state.tx.us/park/parks.htm

This scenic state park covers 2,132 acres of greenery in Sam Houston National Forest. It offers
complete camping facilities on Lake Raven, a marked botany
trail, boating, fishing, and swimming.

Location: Nine miles south of town on the west side of I-45

SAM HOUSTON MEMORIAL MUSEUM COMPLEX

409-294-1832

This town is proud of Sam Houston. Fifteen original acres
belonging to General Sam Houston contain eight buildings: two
period-furnished homes of Houston, a law office, kitchen, blacksmith shop, and gazebo. The museum exhibits Houston's
personal effects and items belonging to Santa Anna when he was
captured at San Jacinto. There's also a gift shop, a small picnic
area, and a pond fed by Houston's original spring.

Location: 1836 Sam Houston Ave.

Hours: Tuesday - Sunday 9:00 a.m. - 4:30 p.m.

SAM HOUSTON STATUE

409-291-9726

It's the world's tallest statue of an American hero. Sculptor
David Adickes, a Huntsville native, used 60,000 pounds of

216

concrete and steel in this towering 66-foot statue of General Sam Houston, visible for more than six miles. Adjacent visitor center.

> The world's tallest statue of an American hero is that of Sam Houston near Huntsville.

Location: I-45 south of town, exit 109

TEXAS PRISON MUSEUM

800-289-0389 or 409-295-8113

Maybe the kids would like to see what used to happen to criminals in Texas. See old ball-and-chains, Bonnie and Clyde's rifles, a cell replica, and "Old Sparky," the state's electric chair (used between 1924-1964). You'll also learn fascinating tales of characters, both the good guys and bad, at the only museum of its kind in Texas.

Location: 1113 12th St.

Hours: Tuesday - Friday noon - 5:00 p.m., Saturday 9:00 a.m. - 5:00 p.m., Sunday noon - 5:00 p.m.

Admission: $2/adult, $1.50/seniors, $1/children 13-18, free under 13

KOUNTZE

BIG THICKET NATIONAL PRESERVE

409-246-2337
http://www.nps.gov/bith/

The area known as the Big Thicket is basically where the southwestern desert meets the eastern hardwood swamps and coastal prairies meet the northern piney woods. Over 96,000 acres comprise this national preserve for the preservation of extremely

diverse plant communities, a considerable number of bird spe-
cies, and a wide variety of wildlife.

The Big Thicket Information Station offers interpretive panels,
along with details and information on trails and boating.

Location: Seven miles north of Kountze on FM 420

Hours: Open daily except Christmas

LIVINGSTON

505 N. Drew
409-327-4929
http://www.livingston.net/chamber/

ALABAMA-COUSHATTA INDIAN RESERVATION

800-444-3507 or 409-563-4391

Deep in the dense, wooded area known as the Big Thicket lived
the Alabama and Coushatta Indians, a southern forest tribe. Sam
Houston, a staunch friend of the Indians, influenced the creation
of the reservation in the 1850s. Visit the Living Indian Village
where tribal members demonstrate traditional skills used to
make jewelry, baskets, and leather items. Watch colorful tribal
dances, tour Big Thicket in a swamp buggy or on the miniature
railroad. There's also a museum and craft shop and a restaurant
that offers traditional Indian foods as well as customary fare and
pit-cooked barbecue. Camping areas, a nice fishing lake, and
swimming are available.

Location: About halfway between Livingston and Woodville on
U.S. 190

Hours: June - August:
Monday - Saturday
9:00 a.m. - 6:00 p.m.,
Sunday 12:30 - 6:00
p.m.; and March -
May and September
weekends only;
closed entirely
December - February

Admission: Fee for
tour

**Alabama-Coushatta
Powwow Princess Fawn
Bullock**
Photo courtesy of
Alabama-Coushatta Tribe
of Texas

LAKE LIVINGSTON STATE PARK
http://www.tpwd.state.tx.us/park/parks.htm

Among dense pine and hardwood forests, multi-use
campsites, screened shelters, and restrooms/showers are available on 640 acres on the eastern shoreline of Lake Livingston.
Activities include boating, fishing, swimming, water skiing, hiking, and nature trails; other facilities include boat ramps, a
bait-house store, gas, and floating docks.

Location: About seven miles southwest of town

MOSCOW

DINOSAUR GARDENS

409-398-4565

What does a saber-tooth tiger sound like? Hear sounds of the smilodon (saber-tooth tiger), as well as other creatures as life-size replicas of dinosaurs "come alive" along a 1,000-foot forest path.

Location: U.S. 59 near FM 62

Hours: June - Labor Day: daily 10:00 a.m. - 6:00 p.m.; September - October and March on weekends 12:30 - 5:30 p.m.; closed November - February

NEDERLAND

WINDMILL MUSEUM

409-722-0279

Built to honor the Dutch heritage of this town, the Windmill Museum contains artifacts of the city's history as well as mementos of country-western singer Tex Ritter.

Location: 1500 block of Boston Ave.

Hours: March - Labor Day: Tuesday - Sunday 1:00 - 5:00 p.m.; rest of the year open Thursday - Sunday 1:00 - 5:00 p.m.

PASADENA

ARMAND BAYOU NATURE CENTER

281-474-2551

This 2500-acre nature preserve is at the southern end of the city, very close to Space Center Houston (see Clear Lake). Located in the largest migratory bird route in North America, it hosts over 220 species of birds and over 350 species of wildlife. See a bird blind with interpretive material, over five miles of trails, and a turn-of-the-century farm. Demonstrations and guided walks on weekends.

Location: 8500 Bay Area Blvd., 7 miles east of I-45

Hours: Wednesday - Saturday 9:00 a.m. - 5:00 p.m., Sunday noon - 5:00 p.m.; closed Monday, Tuesday, and major holidays

SPRING

SPLASH TOWN WATERPARK

281-355-3300
http://www.neosoft.com/~splashtn/

Want to wear out the kids? Bring them to this hugely popular waterpark. It's the largest in the state with more than fifty rides, slides, and attractions. The newest ride, "Wild Water Works Factory" draws thrill-seekers from all over. Court County Fair provides a mini-midway of games and prizes. There's live entertainment and special events throughout the season. Wild Wave Pool, Tree House Island Adventure, Kids Kountry, Texas Freefall—Splash Town Waterpark is a definitely a family attraction.

Location: I-35, at the Louetts Rd. exit

Hours: Daily June - August; weekends in April and September

TEXAS AIR ACES

800-544-2237 or 281-379-2237

"Wannabe" pilots can try their hands in air combat. It's the real thing, not a simulator. Amateur aces fly in the front seat of a T-34A while an air combat instructor supervises the mission from the rear seat. A videotape of the mission is included. Flight experience not required; must be at least 4-feet 8-inches to fly. Reservations required.

Location: D.W. Hooks Airport, 8319 Thora Lane #A-5

SUGAR LAND

IMPERIAL SUGAR COMPANY

800-727-8427

Observe the process of sugar manufacturing in one of the few cane sugar refineries in the U.S.

Hours: Tours are conducted daily at 10:00 a.m. and 2:00 p.m.

WOODVILLE

ALABAMA-COUSHATTA INDIAN RESERVATION—see: LIVINGSTON

HERITAGE VILLAGE

409-283-2272

This open-air display preserves Texas' past in an unusual setting. The Village features old buildings, shops, homes, and vehicles, plus pictures, historical documents, maps, and records of everyday life from pioneer days through the Roaring Twenties. The old schoolhouse now houses the Pickett House restaurant that serves family-style meals daily in the summer.

Location: One mile west on U.S. 190

Hours: Village open daily 9:00 a.m. - 5:00 p.m.; Restaurant hours vary

South & Gulf Coast

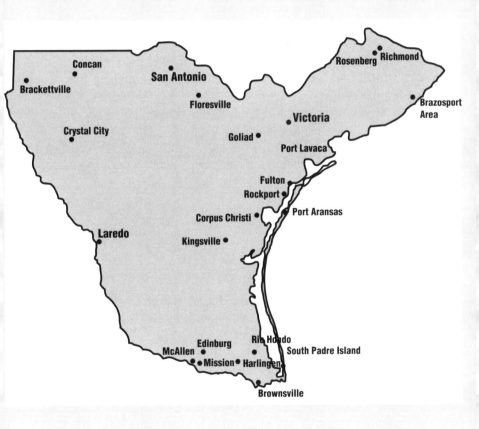

Concan

Brackettville

San Antonio

Floresville

Crystal City

Goliad

Victoria

Port Lavaca

Rosenberg   Richmond

Brazosport
Area

Fulton

Rockport

Corpus Christi

Port Aransas

Laredo

Kingsville

Rio Hondo

Edinburg

McAllen

Mission   Harlingen

South Padre Island

Brownsville

BRACKETVILLE

ALAMO VILLAGE

830-563-2580

How many times have you seen the 1959 John Wayne movie *The Alamo*? This is where it was filmed! Now there's a family recreation center built around the movie set, which was one of the largest and most complete ever constructed in the U.S. The Alamo replica overlooks a complete frontier village of the 1800s—a cantina-restaurant, trading post, Indian store, authentic stage depot, old-time jail, bank, saddle shop, and other structures typical of the Old West. During the summer visitors see regular country-western shows that are often interrupted by shoot-outs between frontier lawmen and desperados. The set is still used for movies, television, and commercials.

Location: Seven miles north of town on RM 674

Hours: Opens daily at 9:00 a.m.

FORT CLARK SPRINGS

800-937-1590
http://www.fortclark.com/main.html

Fort Clark is a privately maintained frontier fort. Today, on the site of the historic fort, is Fort Clark Springs, a resort and leisure living community open to the public. It offers a restaurant, RV park, 9- and18-hole golf courses, a huge spring-fed swimming pool, tennis courts, and nature trails. Overnight accommodations are in stone cavalry barracks transformed into modern motel rooms with private baths. Of course, you'll find a nice military museum, too, and a National Register Historic District preserving a significant place in the history of our nation.

BRAZOSPORT AREA

(Angleton, Brazoria, Clute, Freeport, Jones Creek,
Lake Jackson, Oyster Creek, Quintana Beach, Richwood,
Surfside Beach, and West Columbia)
Brazosport Convention & Visitors Council
888-477-2505 or 409-265-2505
http://www.brazosport.org/

BRAZORIA NATIONAL WILDLIFE REFUGE

409-849-6062

Located on more than 42,000 acres on the Gulf Intracoastal
Waterway, this is a nesting area for mottled ducks and the wintering grounds of snow geese. Almost 250 bird species have
been identified. There's a six-mile self-guided auto tour and hiking trail and access by boat for fishing and crabbing in specific
areas. Before visiting, contact the headquarters.

QUINTANA BEACH COUNTY PARK

800-872-7578 or 409-849-5711

This county park offers exceptional recreational
facilities on a picturesque island. Day-use facilities
include paved parking, shaded pavilions, restrooms, showers,
multi-level fishing pier, and a playground. Elevated boardwalks,
all with wheelchair ramps, connect several of the areas. RV
facilities include over fifty camping sites, full hookups, a dump
station, bathhouse with restrooms, showers, and laundry
facilities.

Location: From Texas 288 in Freeport, take FM 1495 south 1.7
miles, then County Road 723 east 3 miles to the park entrance

SAN BERNARD NATIONAL WILDLIFE REFUGE

Southwest of Lake Jackson, snow and blue geese winter in this 24,000-acre refuge between Cedar Lake Creek and the San Bernard River on the Intracoastal Waterway. Dozens of other bird species nest in the area. For information about access and fishing, contact headquarters at Brazoria Wildlife Refuge above.

SEA CENTER TEXAS

409-292-0100

Everyone will enjoy a visit to this combination marine development, aquarium, and education center. The complex includes the marine fisheries center, a saltwater marsh demonstration project, and a visitor's center. Kids especially like the 24-foot "touch tank," with displays of marine life, and enormous aquariums.

Location: Plantation Dr. and Medical Dr. in Lake Jackson

Hours: Tuesday - Friday 9:00 a.m. - 4:00 p.m., Saturday 10:00 a.m. - 5:00 p.m., Sunday 1:00 - 4:00 p.m. Hatchery tours by reservation only.

BROWNSVILLE

http://brownsville.org/

VISITOR INFORMATION CENTER

800-626-2639 or 956-546-3721

Get detailed local information, maps, and tourist literature, as well as information on visiting Matamoros, Mexico, just across the Rio Grande. Historic trolley sightseeing tours start here.

Location: North Brownsville, at U.S. 77/83 (FM 802 exit)

> Brownsville is Texas' southermost city.

Hours: Monday - Saturday 8:00 a.m. - 5:00 p.m., Sunday 9:00 a.m. - 4:00 p.m.; closed major holidays

CONFEDERATE AIR FORCE: RIO GRANDE VALLEY WING

956-541-8585

This museum features WW II memorabilia, uniforms, artifacts, and a video presentation. Numerous fully operational vintage aircraft from WW II and the Korean Conflict are displayed.

Location: Brownsville/South Padre Island International Airport

Hours: Monday - Saturday 9:00 a.m. - 5:00 p.m., Sunday noon - 4:00 p.m.

GLADYS PORTER ZOO

956-546-2177
http://www.gpz.org/

Visit one of the top rated zoos in the country! A unique concept presents virtually all the animals in open exhibits amid natural waterways and vegetation. The zoo exhibits over 1,550 specimens representing some 420 species, 47 of which are listed as endangered.

All facilities are accessible by wheelchair. Strollers, wheelchairs, and wagons are available for rent at the Zoofari Gift Shop.

New additions and special exhibits are always worth checking out. Permanent sections of the zoo include:

- Tropical America: jaguars, Galapagos tortoises, black-necked swans, flamingos, spider monkeys, and Cuban crocodiles

- Indo-Australia: orangutans, grey kangaroos, kookaburras, wallabies, and black swans

- Asia: Sumatran tigers, guars, pileated gibbons, sarus crane, Indian blue peafowl, and Bactrian camels

- Africa: reticulated giraffes, elephants, zebras, lions, gorillas, chimpanzee, and one of the rarest animals in the world, the Jentink's duiker

- Children's Zoo and Nursery: allows children to interact with Nigerian dwarf goats, miniature mules, and domestic chickens

- Herpetarium and Aquatic Wing: large collection of lizards, turtles, snakes, Gila monsters, and rare crocodilians, along with both fresh and salt water fish from around the world

Location: Ringgold and Sixth St.

Hours: Open daily at 9:00 a.m.

Admission: $6/adults, $4.75/seniors, $3/children, 2 and under free

PORT OF BROWNSVILLE

This deep-water seaport is connected to the Gulf of Mexico by a 17-mile ship channel. The port is home to more than 250 businesses. One of the largest floating dry-docks in the U.S. is alongside the 42-foot deep port, which hosts ships from foreign lands, as well as a large fleet of shrimp boats.

Location: Northeast of town off Texas 48

TROLLEY TOURS

956-546-3721

Step aboard a replica of a turn-of-the-century trolley for a two-hour narrated tour of historic Brownsville, including the city's attractions, the historic downtown area, and a stop at one of the museums. Take the tour of the world-class Port of Brownsville, which includes a detailed look at the seaport and a stop at the

Port Administration Building. Trolley's are equipped with wheel-chair lifts and are fully handicapped accessible.

Location: Tours start and end at the Visitor Information Center at U.S. 77/83 and FM 802

Admission: $7/adults, $3.50/seniors, children 12 and under, students, physically impaired, and Medicare card holders

CONCAN

GARNER STATE PARK
800-792-1112 or 830-232-6132
http://www.tpwd.state.tx.us/park/parks.htm

This popular family-oriented recreational park is located on the Frio River in an exceptionally scenic area of the Hill Country. Tubing on the Frio is unparalleled. Others prefer canoeing, swimming, fishing, hiking, picnicking, seasonal miniature golf and paddleboat rental, and just enjoying nature at its best. Limited accommodations are available in comfortable stone and timber cabins. A camping area provides shaded sites for tents or trailers, screened shelters, and restrooms with showers. There's also a grocery store and a snack bar/restaurant in the summer.

Location: Ten miles north of Concan off U.S. 83, entrance one half mile east on FM 1050

REAGAN WELLS RANCH
800-277-6265 or 830-232-6662
http://www.reaganwells.com

This former boys' home is now a terrific facility for family fun. A variety of accommodations are offered, as well as river access, an enormous

covered and lighted pavilion for basketball and tennis, volleyball courts, horseshoes, hayrides, a playground, game room, and plenty of wildlife viewing and nature trails.

Location: On the Dry Frio River about ten miles from Concan on FM 1051

Reagan Wells Ranch—Children feeding longhorns
Photo courtesy of Reagan Wells Ranch, photo by Steve Crozier

CORPUS CHRISTI

Convention & Visitors Bureau
1201 N. Shoreline Blvd.—800-678-6232 or 512-881-1888
Visitor Center
6667 Texas 77 at IH 37—512-241-1464
Visitor Center
14252 South Padre Island Dr.—800-766-BEACH or
512-949-8743 http://www.cctexas.org/cvb/welcome.htm

CORPUS CHRISTI ZOO

512-814-8000

Kids can meet dozens of barnyard friends at Kidz Zoo, the largest children's petting zoo in the country. The zoo also exhibits an excellent collection of wildlife species, exotic birds, and reptiles.

Location: County Road 33

Hours: Tuesday - Sunday 10:00 a.m. - 6:00 p.m.

Admission: $5/adults, $3/children, discounts for seniors and military

INTERNATIONAL KITE MUSEUM

512-883-7456

Kites are for kids! Not necessarily, as you'll learn at this fascinating museum that traces the history of kites from earliest Chinese kites more than 2,000 years ago. Kites have also been used throughout history in scientific discoveries and warfare. Visit the kite shop, then "go fly your kite" on Corpus Christi Beach.

Location: 3200 Surfside in the Best Western-Sandy Shores Hotel

Hours: Daily 10:00 a.m. - 6:00 p.m.

Admission: FREE

PADRE ISLAND NATIONAL SEASHORE—see also: SOUTH PADRE ISLAND

512-937-2621
http://www.nps.gov/pais/

Each end of this narrow, 110-mile sand island is developed with parks and resorts, but in between the National Seashore preserves an 80-mile pristine stretch of white sand beaches and picturesque windswept dunes. It's one of the longest stretches of undeveloped ocean beach in the U.S. Swim, fish, hike, beachcomb for shells, surf, picnic, or just enjoy watching the birds and viewing scenic grassland landscapes. Facilities include a visitor center with gifts and concessions, bathhouse, and picnic area.

PLAYLAND AT THE BEACH

512-884-7251

This outdoor family park features Grand Prix go-cart races, bumper boats, bumper cars, children's playground, and a large game room.

Location: 3001 Seagull Blvd.

Hours: Open seasonally, weather permitting

TEXAS STATE AQUARIUM

800-477-GULF or 512-881-1200
http://www.txstateaq.com/

Enter through cascades of water above a glass-enclosed tunnel as you begin your undersea adventure. The aquarium features close-up views and living displays of the wonders of the Gulf of

Mexico. "The Wonderful World of Sherman's Lagoon" features Jim Toomey's cartoon characters who guide you through the exhibit and explain lagoons, barrier reefs, and the animals that inhabit them. Conservation Cove is home to sea turtles, including endangered species.

Location: 2710 N. Shoreline Blvd. on Corpus Christi Beach

Hours: Monday - Saturday 9:00 a.m. - 5:00 p.m., Sunday 10:00 a.m. - 5:00 p.m.; extended hours in the summer

Admission: $8/adults, $5.75/children ages 12-17, seniors, and active duty military (with valid ID), $4.50/children under 12, and free for children under 4

Texas State Aquarium
Photo by Debbie Witcher

USS LEXINGTON MUSEUM ON THE BAY
800-LADY-LEX or 512-888-4873

Adjacent to the Texas State Aquarium, this vintage aircraft carrier is now a floating naval museum. You can choose from five tour routes, then visit the exhibits, and for those who want to experience the sensation of flight, there's a high-tech flight simulator. Helicopter rides depart from the flight deck.

Location: 2914 N. Shoreline Blvd.

Hours: Daily 9:00 a.m. - 5:00 p.m.; extended hours in the summer

Admission: $8/adults, $6.50/seniors and military (with valid ID), $3/children ages 4-17, and free for children under 3

WORLD OF DISCOVERY
512-883-2862

An all-day adventure, this complex includes the Corpus Christi Museum of Science and Natural History, the Ships of Christopher Columbus, and the Xeriscape Learning Center and Design Garden. The excellent natural history museum contains Gulf Coast shells and artifacts, wildlife dioramas, pictures, and hands-on exhibits. The Ships of Christopher Columbus are replicas of the famous ships, authentic in detail and construction, built by the Spanish government to commemorate the 500th anniversary of Columbus's voyage.

Location: 1900 N. Chaparral

Hours: Monday - Saturday 10:00 a.m. - 5:00 p.m., Sunday noon - 5:00 p.m.

Admission: $8/adults, $6.50/seniors and military (with valid ID, $7/youth ages 13-17, $4/children ages 5-12, free for children under 5

CRYSTAL CITY

POPEYE STATUE

Get your picture taken with Popeye the Sailor Man. This whimsical salute to the area's spinach crop is downtown on the town square.

EDINBURG

Chamber of Commerce
210-383-4974
http://www.edinburg.com/chamber/

SHERIFF'S POSSE RODEO

Every Saturday evening, rodeo cowboys demonstrate calf roping, bull riding, and quarter horse racing at the rodeo arena. It's free to watch, except during full-performance rodeos.

Location: Two miles south of Edinburg via U.S. 281, then a half mile west on Wisconsin Rd.

Admission: FREE

SUPERSPLASH

800-667-1456 or 956-318-3286

SuperSplash Adventure features lush, tropical landscaping with palm trees, rose gardens, ferns, flower gardens, bamboo groves, and fountains. The 25-acre water park features a kids area entitled Castaway Cove with a multi-level water playhouse, water cannons, water valves and jets, sprayers, showers, and geysers. For the toddlers, Kids Cove has a shallow pool with soft foam

water slides, water bubblers, and ticklers. Mammoth River is for the truly adventurous.

The park features two wave pools, tube rides, and a 16-foot wide "Adventure River." Pizza, hamburgers, tacos, sweets and treats, and even health foods are available throughout the park. A gift shop has souvenirs and items you may have forgotten to bring.

Location: 1616 S. Raul Longoria Rd., just off U.S. 281

Hours: May - October

Admission: $16.95/adults, $12.95/children (all-day)

FLORESVILLE

PROMISED LAND DAIRY

830-216-7182

Ever taste strawberry milk? Peach milk? Have you ever seen glass milk bottles? This farm is home to one of the largest registered all-Jersey herds in the world. The dairy also makes ice cream the old-fashioned way and uses only Texas-grown fruits and nuts when possible. Kids love to tour the dairy and feed and pet the animals in the petting barnyard. There's an ice cream parlor and gift shop as well as a very nice restaurant.

Location: South of San Antonio, three miles west of Floresville on Texas 97

Hours: Tours daily

GOLIAD

Chamber of Commerce
205 S. Market
800-848-8674 or 512-645-3563
http://www.goliad.org/

GOLIAD STATE HISTORICAL PARK

512-645-3405
http://www.tpwd.state.tx.us/park/parks.htm

This park, located on the San Antonio River, features a restored mission, excellent interpretive displays, plus a camping and picnic area, restrooms, and fishing spots. A junior-size Olympic swimming pool, across the highway and not a part of the state park, is operated by the city.

Location: One mile south of U.S. 183

PRESIDIO LA BAHIA

This is Texas history at its best! As the Spanish built missions on the frontier, a presidio (military fort) was usually built nearby to protect the mission. Such was Presidio Santa Maria del Loreto de la Bahia, established in 1749. It is now the finest fully restored example of a complete Spanish presidio in Texas. The chapel is still used regularly for religious services. A museum houses objects discovered during the restoration, memorabilia of the Texas Revolution, and artifacts that indicate nine levels of civilization at the site.

Location: Two miles south off U.S. 183

Hours: Daily 9:00 a.m. - 4:45 p.m.; closed major holidays

HARLINGEN

Chamber of Commerce
311 East Tyler
800-531-7346 or 956-423-5440
http://www.harlingen.com/

TEXAS TRAVEL INFORMATION CENTER

Professional bilingual travel counselors offer free maps, literature, and expert help. Free tourism video shows and lavish
tropical landscaping—great place for a break to stretch your
legs.

Location: Intersection of U.S. 77/83 in town

Hours: Open daily 8:00 a.m. - 5:00 p.m.; closed major holidays

RIO GRANDE VALLEY HISTORICAL MUSEUM COMPLEX

956-430-8500

This complex includes three historical structures, a wide variety
of exhibits, a video theater, and a museum store. Paso Real
Stagecoach Inn, circa 1850, displays period furnishings; the
original Harlingen Hospital exhibits vintage medical equipment
and dental and medical offices of the 1920s; and the Lon C. Hill
Home, built by the "father" of Harlingen, displays many original
family possessions.

Location: Loop 499 at Boxwood and Raintree St.

Hours: Wednesday - Saturday 10:00 .m. - 4:00 p.m., Sunday 1:00
- 4:00 p.m.

KINGSVILLE

Visitors Centers:
US 77 at Corral Street
King Ave. at Third Street
800-333-5032 or 512-592-8516
http://www.kingsville.org/

KING RANCH

512-592-8055
http://www.king-ranch.com/

One of the most famous ranches in the country, this National Historic Landmark was established in 1853 when Captain Richard King purchased 75,000 acres that had been part of a Spanish land grant. Today the ranch comprises 825,000 acres spread over four counties. The now-famous Santa Gertrudis breed, the first strain of beef cattle originating in the Western Hemisphere, was developed here. A Visitor Center features an informative video on the ranch's operation and offers an audio tape to accompany a self-guided driving tour.

Location: Just west of Kingsville off Texas 141

Hours: Monday - Saturday 9:00 a.m. - 4:00 p.m., Sunday noon - 5:00 p.m.; Ranch tour times vary with the seasons

KING RANCH MUSEUM

512-595-1881

Collections of antique coaches, vintage cars, saddles, and other historic ranch items are displayed in a restored downtown ice plant. Partially handicapped accessible.

Location: 405 N. Sixth St.

Hours: Monday - Saturday noon - 4:00 p.m., Sunday 1:00 - 5:00 p.m.; closed New Year's Day, Easter, Thanksgiving, Christmas Eve, and Christmas Day

Admission: $4/adults, $2.50/children 5-12

KING RANCH SADDLE SHOP

800-282-KING or 512-595-5761

Mr. King could not find quality saddles and leather goods, so he began operating his own saddlery shop more than 120 years ago. Through the years, governors, presidents, and foreign heads of state have been outfitted from the shop. Today visitors may buy a variety of quality leather goods.

Location: 201 E. Kleberg in the historic downtown Raglands Building

Hours: Monday - Saturday 10:00 a.m. - 6:00 p.m.

PARKS

City parks include swimming pools, tennis courts, picnic areas, and playgrounds. Dick Kleberg Park, off Loop 428 near the south edge of the city beside a lazy creek, features picnic tables, grills, and a swimming pool.

LAREDO

Laredo Convention & Visitors Bureau
501 San Agustin
800-361-3360 or 956-795-2200
http://www.visitlaredo.com

LAREDO CHILDREN'S MUSEUM

956-725-2299

Meet new friends Yippee, Rudie, and Booboo, as they guide you through the museum. Yippee loves history and culture; Rudie is into art; and Booboo is a science nut. Through hands-on experimentation and exploration, the innovative museum encourages the explorer and inventor in all children.

Location: On the campus of Laredo Junior College.

Hours: Thursday - Saturday 10:00 a.m. - 5:00 p.m., Sunday 1:00 - 5:00 p.m.

MCALLEN

Chamber of Commerce
10 N. Broadway
800-250-2591
http://www.mcallen.org

MCALLEN INTERNATIONAL MUSEUM

956-682-1564

This museum presents exhibits, educational programs, and special activities relating to art and science, in addition to a collection of art and Mexican arts and crafts.

Location: 1900 Nolana at Bicentennial

Hours: Tuesday - Saturday 9:00 a.m. - 5:00 p.m., Sunday 1:00 - 5:00 p.m.

Admission: $2/adults, $1/students 13 and over and seniors, 50¢/students 12 and under

MOUNTASIA

956-682-9761

Kids of all ages enjoy this fun-filled park. Games include minia-ture golf, bumper cars, bumper boats, go-carts, a video arcade, and restaurant.

Location: On U.S. 83

Hours: Monday - Thursday 1:00 - 11:00 p.m., Friday 1:00 p.m. - midnight, Saturday 11:00 a.m. - midnight, Sunday noon - 11:00 p.m.

VALLEY DRIVE-IN THEATRE

956-682-8201

Treat the kids to a memory from your past—the drive-in theater. One of the few still operating in Texas, the Valley Drive-In sometimes shows three movies in an evening.

MISSION

LOS EBANOS FERRY

The only existing hand-operated ferry on U.S.-Mexican border, it carries three cars at a time. Yes, men actually pull cables to make it go. It's named for a grove of ebony trees (ebanos) where it crosses the Rio Grande.

Location: Fifteen miles southwest of town via U.S. 83, three miles south on FM 886

Hours: Operates daily 8:00 a.m. - 4:00 p.m.

PORT ARANSAS

Convention & Visitors Bureau
421 W. Cotter
800-452-6278 or 512-749-5919
http://www.portaransas.org/

MUSTANG ISLAND STATE PARK

512-883-2862 or 512-749-5246
http://www.tpwd.state.tx.us/park/parks.htm

This popular park has nearly 4,000 acres of sand dunes, sea oats, and five miles of Gulf beach frontage offering the best of seaside camping, surfing, fishing, swimming, and shell collecting. Facilities include multi-use campsites with hookups plus a large beach area for primitive camping, dump station, picnic arbors, restrooms, showers, nature trail, and fish-cleaning station. It's home to abundant shore and migratory birds.

Location: About 14 miles south of Port Aransas on Texas 361

UNIVERSITY OF TEXAS MARINE SCIENCE INSTITUTE

512-749-6729

This is a great introduction to oceanography. The laboratory and research facility displays Gulf marine life and plants.

Location: Along the ship channel between Mustang and San Jose Islands

Hours: Weekdays 8:00 a.m.- noon, 1:00 - 5:00 p.m.

PORT LAVACA

LIGHTHOUSE BEACH AND BIRD SANCTUARY

Stroll on a beautiful sandy beach with waterfront camping sites, swimming pool and playgrounds. The Formosa Wetland Walkway and Alcoa Bird Tower provide visitors a place to watch the birds.

PORT LAVACA CAUSEWAY STATE FISHING PIER

512-552-5311

Replaced by a modern bridge, this old highway causeway is now a popular lighted fishing pier extending 3,202 feet into Lavaca Bay. You can swim, go boating, or go saltwater fishing. Facilities include snack bar, bait stand, and restrooms. Port Lavaca City Park at base of pier has boat ramp, picnicking, and recreational vehicle facilities.

Location: Alongside Texas 35 causeway

RICHMOND/ROSENBERG

BRAZOS BEND STATE PARK

http://tpwd.state.tx.us/park/parks.htm

Like other state parks, this one provides areas for tent and RV camping, picnic sites, screened shelters, restrooms, showers, fishing pier, hike and bike trails, and wildlife observation platforms. Almost 5,000 acres of Gulf Coastal Plain include Brazos River bottomlands, live-oak woodlands, lakes and marshes with abundant wildlife. The George Observatory within the park features a 36-inch telescope and is open to the public for stargazing on Saturday nights.

Location: Access via FM 762, 20 miles south

GEORGE RANCH HISTORICAL PARK

281-545-9212

Experience Texas history at this 470-acre living history site.
Visit an 1820s farmstead or an 1890s Victorian mansion staffed
by costumed guides. Watch demonstrations of pioneer crafts and
skills. The ranch is operational; see cowboys working cattle in a
1930s working ranch area. The ranch is associated with the Ft.
Bend Museum.

Location: Eight miles south of Richmond on FM 762

Hours: April - mid-December: Saturday - Sunday 10:00 a.m. -
5:00 p.m.

RIO HONDO

LAGUNA ATASCOSA NATIONAL WILDLIFE REFUGE

Thousands of waterfowl winter at this 46,000-acre refuge. It's at
the southern end of the Central Flyway and includes 7,000 acres
of marshland. Driving routes and walking routes lead past viewing areas, and a visitor center features wildlife exhibits and a
picnic area.

Location: Seven miles east to intersection FM 106/ FM 1847

Hours: Open daylight hours except major holidays

THE TEXAS AIR MUSEUM

210-748-2112

The Texas Air Museum presents the history of aviation with
exhibits of more than thirty aircraft. This is one of the few

remaining aviation museums that has full restoration facilities. You can watch several planes actually being restored.

Location: One mile east on FM 106

Hours: Monday - Saturday 9:00 a.m. - 4:00 p.m.

Admission: $4/adults, $2/children 12-16, $1/children 11 and under

ROCKPORT/FULTON

Chamber of Commerce
404 S. Broadway St.
800-242-0071 or 512-729-6445
http://www.rockport-fulton.org/

ARANSAS NATIONAL WILDLIFE REFUGE
512-286-3559

Renowned as the principal wintering ground for the near-extinct whooping crane, this refuge is on a broad peninsula across the bay northeast of Rockport. A Wildlife Interpretive Center features mounted specimens, a slide show on whooping cranes, and literature. This is a great place for observing nature, hiking, and photography. Please use the designated public-use roads, trails, observation towers, and picnic areas.

Location: Refuge headquarters are about 35 miles northeast of Rockport via Texas 35 north, FM 774 east, and FM 2040 south

Hours: Open daylight hours

GOOSE ISLAND STATE PARK

512-729-2858

http://www.tpwd.state.tx.us/park/parks.htm

Goose Island is home to the "Big Tree," an immense live oak certified as the largest in Texas, estimated to be 1,000 years old. On a peninsula between Copano and St. Charles Bays, this park offers a children's play area, restrooms, showers, picnic sites, fishing pier, fish cleaning table, boat ramp, and unsupervised beach for bay swimming; tent and trailer camping is permitted.

Location: About 12 miles north of Rockport via Texas 35 and Park Road 13

TEXAS MARITIME MUSEUM

512-729-1271

Experience the rich maritime heritage of Texas. Learn how Texas has relied on the sea throughout history with changing exhibits, interactive displays, and educational public programming.

Location: 1202 Navigation Circle across from the picturesque Rockport Harbor

Hours: Tuesday - Saturday 10:00 a.m. - 4:00 p.m., Sunday 1:00 - 4:00 p.m.; closed major holidays

Admission: $4/adults, $2/children 4-12, free for children under 4

SAN ANTONIO

800-447-3372
http://www.sanantoniocvb.com

The Alamo City is the state's number-one tourist destination. Due to the immense variety and number of kid-friendly attractions in this metropolitan area, only a few are listed, and you're encouraged to get a copy of the book *Exploring San Antonio with Children* and visit the local Visitor Information Center for more detailed information.

> **Tip:**
>
> Call 800-447-3372 and request a S.A.V.E. (San Antonio Vacation Experience) booklet offering discounts at various hotels and attractions.

THE ALAMO

Stand where the Texas heroes stood! Mission San Antonio de Valero, later to become famous as "The Alamo," was established in 1718, the first of five Spanish missions founded in San Antonio.

Location: Alamo Plaza in the heart of downtown

Hours: Open Monday - Saturday 9:00 a.m. - 5:30 p.m., Sunday 10:00 a.m. - 5:30 p.m.

Admission: FREE, donations welcomed

BRACKENRIDGE PARK—see also: SAN ANTONIO ZOO

210-736-9534

Ride the Skyride or the Brackenridge Eagle, a one-fifth-scale model of a diesel train for a view of the city's largest park. It includes rustic stone bridges and winding walks, gleaming pools, a Japanese Sunken Garden, countless picnic areas, paddleboats, riding stables, and bridle paths. Sometimes the Sunken Gardens Theater presents entertainment.

Location: 3500 N. St. Mary's

El Mercado (The Market)

This is the place to go for a souvenir sombrero. El Mercado typifies a market from the interior of Mexico and offers local handicrafts and imports including wrought iron, pottery, woodcarvings, leather and straw goods; colorful stalls feature farm-fresh produce.

Location: Santa Rosa and Commerce St.

Jungle Jim's Playland

210-490-9595

Kids have a blast at this indoor, air-conditioned mini-amusement park. Parents may ride the roller coasters, Ferris wheel, bumper cars, flying planes, and other rides with small children. There are also two "soft" playground areas and lots of snack foods like pizza, hot dogs, and popcorn.

Location: 13311 San Pedro Ave.

Hemisfair Park

Hold your breath, but don't close your eyes! You won't want to miss the panoramic view as you ride the outside glass elevator to the top of the 750-foot Tower of the Americas. The site of the 1968 Texas World's Fair, the park is now an area of downtown entertainment and recreation. There's a sky-high dining room plus an observation deck at the top of the Tower. A very nice children's playground area is located on the beautifully landscaped Hemisfair grounds.

Tower elevator fee: $3/adults, $1/children 4-11

HERTZBERG CIRCUS MUSEUM

210-207-7810

Calling all "big top" fans to "The Greatest Show on Earth" in miniature. Mr. and Mrs. Tom Thumb's carriage, costumes, circus posters, photographs, and big-top memorabilia are displayed in this unusual museum. Circus videos are shown throughout the day, and special events such as magicians, storytellers, and puppeteers are scheduled frequently.

Location: 210 W. Market St.

Hours: June - Labor Day: Monday - Saturday 10:00 a.m. - 5:00 p.m., Sundays, holidays 1:00 - 5:00 p.m.

Admission: $2.50/adults, $1/children 3-12

IMAX THEATER

800-354-IMAX or 210-225-4629

Alamo . . . The Price of Freedom is a 45-minute docudrama, which tells the story of the 189 defenders of the Alamo who chose to die for freedom. What a spectacle to watch on IMAX's six-story-tall theater screen.

Location: In Rivercenter Mall, 849 E. Commerce #483

Hours: Daily 9:00 a.m. - 10:00 p.m.

Admission: $7.25/adults, $4.75/children 3-11

LA VILLITA (Little Village)

A restored little Mexican village captures the charm of the past. Amid narrow streets, shaded patios, and authentic adobe houses are small restaurants, specialty shops, and arts and craft shops.

Location: Beside the river in the heart of downtown, bounded by South Alamo and Nueva St.

NATURAL BRIDGE CAVERNS—see: HILL COUNTRY SECTION, NEW BRAUNFELS

NATURAL BRIDGE WILDLIFE RANCH—see: HILL COUNTRY SECTION, NEW BRAUNFELS

> Bracken Cave, Near San Antonio, is home to the world's largest known bat colony.

RIPLEY'S BELIEVE IT OR NOT! MUSEUM

210-224-9299

Where else can you see authentic dinosaur eggs? Explore themed galleries filled with over 500 one-of-a-kind oddities and artifacts from the beautiful and bizarre world famous collection of Robert Ripley.

Location: 301 Alamo Plaza

Admission: $8.95/adults, $5.50/children 4-12

SAN ANTONIO CHILDREN'S MUSEUM

210-212-4453

The first thing you'll see is the soaring "Landmark Climbing Structure" reaching to the museum's mezzanine level. There's lots to see and do in this hands-on museum, designed for children ages two to ten, in the heart of downtown San Antonio.

Location: 305 E. Houston St.

Hours: Tuesday - Saturday 9:00 a.m. - 6:00 p.m., Sunday noon - 5:00 p.m.

Admission: $4, children under 2 free

SAN ANTONIO ZOO—see also: BRACKENRIDGE PARK

210-734-7183
http://www.sazoo-aq.org/

The third largest animal collection in North America presents more than 3,000 animals of over 700 different species in natural habitats. It is a sanctuary for endangered species such as the whooping crane, snow leopard, and white rhino. Other exhibits on the twenty-five landscaped acres include an Australian walkabout to view koalas, kangaroos, and other animals from Down Under, Africa's Rift Valley with African wildlife, two aquariums displaying assorted marine life, and a children's zoo featuring a tropical boat tour. Elephant and camel rides are offered most days during the summer. The zoo offers fun and educational children's programs all year. Wheelchair accessible.

Location: 3903 N. St. Mary's in Brackenridge Park

Hours: Daily 9:30 a.m. - 5:00 p.m. (until 6:30 from April - November)

Admission: $6/adults, $4/children 3-11

SEA WORLD OF TEXAS

210-523-3611

Whoever heard of a "Sea" in the middle of Texas? Well, there is one. It's the world's largest marine life park with more than twenty-five spectacular shows, educational exhibits, rides and family attractions. Loveable dolphins, playful otters, clumsy walruses, and immense killer whales find Texas waters as comfortable as the ocean. Kids can play and splash at Shamu's Happy Harbor and at Lil' Gators Lagoon. Lost Lagoon water adventure area offers a huge wave pool, slides, a palm-studded beach, an alligator habitat, and an aviary. The aviary is filled with lorikeets, a colorful parrot that will eat out of your hand. State-of-the-art animal habitats include the Corral Reef, the Penguin Encounter, and the Marine Mammal Pool.

Kids have a blast on rides such as the Texas Splashdown flume and the Rio Loco river rapids ride. And the "Great White" is well known to roller coaster buffs. Several kiddie rides are adjacent to The Great White Games Center, filled with midway games and the SeaNet laser tag adventure.

Location: Sixteen miles northwest of downtown, off Texas 151 at Ray Ellison Drive and Westover Hills Blvd.

Hours: Weekends and some weekdays in spring; daily during the summer; and weekends in the fall

SIX FLAGS FIESTA TEXAS

800-IS-FIESTA (473-4378)
http://www.sixflags.com/parks/

This 200-acre theme park highlights Texas culture and music in four themed areas:

- Los Festivales: a nonstop fiesta featuring the strong Mexican and Spanish heritage of San Antonio with two theaters and a restaurant

- Crackaxle Canyon: a 1920s boom town, including a narrow gauge railroad and train station, two theaters, the "Rattler," a world-class wooden roller coaster, and a restaurant

- Spassburg: displays the tremendous German influence in the Texas Hill Country with Sangerfest Halle, a restaurant and music hall, early 1900s-style carousel, train station, and children's rides

- Rockville: a salute to Texas in the 1950s with everything from a high school gym to a corner malt shop. "Rockin' at Rockville High" is consistently named one of the top entertainment shows in America.

Fiesta Bay Boardwalk features a 90-foot Ferris wheel, roller skating pavilion, wading pool, paddleboats, and an ADA-approved 18-hole miniature golf course. You'll find dozens of rides, shows, water rides, and activities. New in 1998 is the "Legends in Concert" where impersonators perform as Elvis and other famous celebrities.

Location: Fifteen minutes from downtown off Loop 1604 and I-10, exit 555

Hours: Daily in summer, weekends spring and fall; closed December - February

Admission: $33/adults, $23.50/children, seniors, and physically impared

SPLASHTOWN

210-227-1100

This 18-acre water recreation park features water slides, a huge surf pool, sandy beach, river, and lots of children's activities. Call for hours and rates.

Location: Just north of downtown off I-35 at Splashtown exit

Hours: Open April - September

THE TEXAS ADVENTURE

210-227-8224

A cannon fires and a cannon ball races overhead, muskets shoot and a lampshade across the room falls, the sky erupts with fire. Billed as a "200-seat time machine," this theater is the first of its kind where special effects bring ghost-like images to life reliving the struggle for Texas Independence. Also includes historical displays, a souvenir store, and a snack bar.

Location: 307 Alamo Plaza

Hours: Daily 9:00 a.m. - 10:00 p.m. in summer (9:00 a.m. - 6:00 p.m. in winter)

THE WITTE MUSEUM

210-357-1900
http://wittemuseum.org/

Even if the kids don't ordinarily care for museums, they'll like this one. It has outstanding exhibits of natural history and natural science, dioramas of Texas flora and wildlife. Four early Texas houses and a furnished log cabin were rebuilt on the grounds. The HEB Science Treehouse, beside the San Antonio River, features four levels of hands-on science exhibits just for kids. A fine gift shop is located in the museum.

Location: 3801 Broadway

Hours: Monday - Saturday 10:00 a.m. - 5:00 p.m. (Tuesday until 9:00 p.m.), Sunday noon - 5:00 p.m. Extended summer hours; closed Thanksgiving and Christmas Day

Admission: $5.95/adults, $4.95/seniors 65+, $3.95/children 4-11, children 3 and under free; FREE admission on Tuesdays from 3:00 - 9:00 p.m.

WILLIES GRILL AND ICEHOUSE

210-490-9220

Willies serves super hamburgers, chicken fingers, and salads. Kids eat free Sunday through Thursday. There's a giant outside sandbox and large indoor video game room to entertain them.

Location: 15801 San Pedro Ave

SOUTH PADRE ISLAND

Visitor Center
600 Padre Blvd. (½ mile north of causeway)
800-SO PADRE or 956-761-6433
http://www.sopadre.com/

Dozens of companies offer boat tours, fishing charters, dive charters, beach buggy rentals, parasailing, scuba and snorkeling lessons, windsurfing lessons, and other water related sports and activities. Pick up a list at the Visitor Center.

> The Queen Isabella Causeway is the longest bridge in Texas—2.6 miles.

ISLAND EQUESTRIAN CENTER

800-761-4677 or 956-761-4677

Horses are available for all levels of riders over six years of age. Bring your camera and ride along the beach, especially lovely at sunset. Pony rides for those under six.

JEREMIAH'S

956-761-2131

This small water park has seven water slides, a pollywog pond, video arcade, and snack bar.

Location: 100 Padre Blvd.

Hours: Memorial Day - Labor Day

PADRE ISLAND NATIONAL SEASHORE—see: CORPUS CHRISTI

PARKS

Isla Blanca Park (956-761-5493), at the southernmost tip of the island, consists of a mile of clean white beach along the Gulf of Mexico. Waterfront recreational facilities include picnic and playground areas, fishing jetty, restaurants, full-service marina, water park, 1,000-foot sea walk, boat ramp, camping facilities, and 600 RV sites with full hookups.

Just north of the city, Andy Bowie Park (956-761-2639) features the popular Laguna Madre Nature Trail. Other facilities include beachfront picnic pavilions, children's playground, and ranger station.

SOUTH PADRE ISLAND AQUARIUM

956-761-7067

This small aquarium displays about twenty-five aquatic species indigenous to the Laguna Madre and the Gulf.

Location: 2305 Laguna Blvd.

Hours: Daily 10:00 a.m. - 10:00 p.m.

VICTORIA

RIVERSIDE PARK

Along the Guadalupe River, this park consists of 562 acres of woodland, numerous picnic areas with tables and barbecue pits, playground equipment, and a 27-hole Riverside Golf Course.

The Texas Zoo (in Riverside Park) is devoted exclusively to native Texas species and displays them in a natural environment with no cages.

Hours: Daily 10:00 a.m. - 5:00 p.m.; extended hours in summer

RESOURCES

Texas Travel Information Centers:

Stop at one of the Texas Travel Information Centers at entry points around the state. Each is manned by professional travel counselors and packed with travel literature and maps to make your trip more enjoyable. They are open daily from 8:00 a.m. to 5:00 p.m., except New Year's, Thanksgiving, Christmas Eve, and Christmas Day.

- Amarillo—I-40 at U.S. 287

- Anthony (El Paso)—I-10 at New Mexico state line

- Austin—Capitol Complex Visitors Center at Congress Ave. and 11th

- Denison—U.S. 75 and 69

- Gainesville—I-35 North at U.S. 77

- Harlingen—U.S. 77 and 83

- Langtry—Loop 25 at U.S. 90

- Laredo—I-35 North

- Orange—I-10

- Texarkana—I-30 at Arkansas state line

- Waskom—I-20 at Louisiana state line

- Wichita Falls—I-44 at U.S. 277 and 281

Texas Tourism Division

P.O. Box 12728
Austin, TX 78711
800-888-8TEX
288-page Texas State Travel Guide
http://www.traveltex.com

Travel planning assistance and emergency road condition information:
800-452-9292

Department of Transportation (D.O.T.)
http://www.dot.state.tx.us

Texas Highways magazine (D.O.T. publication)
http://www.texashighways.com

Texas Parks and Wildlife Department
4200 Smith School Rd.
Austin, TX 78744
800-792-1112
State Parks information
http://www.tpwd.state.tx.us/park/parks.htm

USEFUL WEBSITES:

http://www.easttexasguide.com/ - East Texas travel guide

http://www.texassleepaways.com/ - lots of links

http://www.aza.org - American Zoo and Aquarium Association

http://family.disney.com/Local/TX/ - Disney's family travel site; lots of good information, *Family Fun* magazine, current events

http://gotexas.miningco.com/ - good information about vacation planning http://cust2.iamerica.net/coz/texas.htm - Texas Landmarks and Legacies; dozens of links and good information

http://www.texaswest.com/standard-times/rodeo/calendar.htm - West Texas rodeo schedule

http://www.noplacebuttexas.com/ - calendar of events, many links

http://www.yeeha.net/directory/index.html - good resource directory, not just travel—everything about Texas

http://www.texasrails.com/ - Texas railroad information

http://tourtexas.com/tfea/tfea.html - Texas Festivals and Events

http://tourtexas.com/tnta/tnta.html - Texas Nature Tourism Association

http://www.astc.org - science museums across the U.S.

http://travel.org/texas.html - mostly big city information, some links

http://wildtexas.com/ - Texas parks, nature, and travel guide

http://www.intellicast.com/ - good weather site

http://www.parents.com - great site for parents about all subjects, including travel with kids

NEWSMAGAZINE:

Festivals of Texas
2240 Morriss Rd. Suite 110/191
Flower Mound, TX 75028
888-459-2993 or 972-459-2993

This excellent bimonthly publication lists hundreds of celebrations, festivals, and special events around the state. Single copies are complimentary at state visitor centers; annual subscriptions are $13.

Several family travel books are available. Two outstanding ones are:

Family Travel: The Complete Guide by Pamela Lanier; paperback, 320 pages, 1996

Lonely Planet Travel with Children by Maureen Wheeler, paperback, 160 pages, 1995

Index

Index